D0999257

ΑΙΣΧΥΛΟΥ   AESCHYLUS'
Πέρσαι   *Persians*

A Dual Language Edition

Greek Text Edited (1926) by
Herbert Weir Smyth

English Translation and Notes by
Ian Johnston

Edited by
Evan Hayes and Stephen Nimis

FAENUM PUBLISHING
OXFORD, OHIO

Aeschylus Persians: *A Dual Language Edition*
First Edition

© 2017 by Faenum Publishing

ISBN-10: 1940997984
ISBN-13: 9781940997988

Published by Faenum Publishing, Ltd.
Cover Design: Evan Hayes

for Geoffrey (1974-1997)

οἵη περ φύλλων γενεὴ τοίη δὲ καὶ ἀνδρῶν.
φύλλα τὰ μέν τ' ἄνεμος χαμάδις χέει, ἄλλα δέ θ' ὕλη
τηλεθόωσα φύει, ἔαρος δ' ἐπιγίγνεται ὥρη:
ὣς ἀνδρῶν γενεὴ ἣ μὲν φύει ἣ δ' ἀπολήγει.

Generations of men are like the leaves.
In winter, winds blow them down to earth,
but then, when spring season comes again,
the budding wood grows more. And so with men:
one generation grows, another dies away.   (*Iliad* 6)

TABLE OF CONTENTS

Editors' Note vii

Historical Note ix

Aeschylus' *Persians* 1

Notes 123

EDITORS' NOTE

This book presents the Greek text of Aeschylus' *Persians* with a facing English translation. The Greek text is that of Herbert Weir Smyth (1926), which is in the public domain and available as a pdf. This text has also been digitized by the Perseus Project (perseus.tufts.edu). The English translation and accompanying notes are those of Ian Johnston of Vancouver Island University, Nanaimo, BC. This translation is available freely online (records.viu.ca/~johnstoi/). We have reset both texts, making a number of very minor corrections, and placed them on opposing pages. This facing-page format will be useful to those wishing to read the English translation while looking at the Greek version, or vice versa.

Note that some discrepancies exists between the Greek text and English translation. Occasionally readings from other editions of or commentaries on Aeschylus' Greek text are used, accounting for some minor departures from Smyth.

HISTORICAL NOTE

Aeschylus (c.525 BC to c.456 BC) was one of the three great Greek tragic dramatists whose works have survived. Of his many plays, seven still remain. Aeschylus may have fought against the Persians at Marathon (490 BC), and he did so again at Salamis (480 BC). According to tradition, he died from being hit with a tortoise dropped by an eagle. After his death, the Athenians, as a mark of respect, permitted his works to be restaged in their annual competitions.

Aeschylus' play *Persians* was first produced in 472 BC. It is commonly regarded as the oldest surviving play in our traditions.

Persian armies launched two famous invasions against the Greek mainland. The first (in 490 BC) was sponsored by Darius, king of Persia. It ended at the Battle of Marathon close to Athens with a Greek victory, in which the Athenians played the major role. The second Persian expedition (in 480 BC) was sponsored and led by Xerxes, son of Darius, who had succeeded his father as king, after Darius' death.

A major reason for these invasions was to punish Athens for its assistance to Greek cities in Asia Minor and on some of the islands close by, an important part of the Persians' sphere of influence. These cities had close ethnic links to the Greeks, especially to the Athenians, and resented Persian domination. Hence, they were a source of conflict within the Persian Empire.

ΠΕΡΣΑΙ

PERSIANS

ΤΑ ΤΟΥ ΔΡΑΜΑΤΟΣ ΠΡΟΣΩΠΑ

ΑΤΟΣΣΑ

ΑΓΓΕΛΟΣ

ΔΑΡΕΙΟΣ

ΞΕΡΞΗΣ

ΧΟΡΟΣ

DRAMATIS PERSONAE

ATOSSA: queen of Persia, mother of Xerxes, wife of Darius.[1]

MESSENGER: a soldier with Xerxes' army.

DARIUS: a ghost, father of Xerxes, once king of Persia.

XERXES: king of Persia, son of Darius and Atossa.

CHORUS: elder statesmen of Persia.

Πέρσαι

Τάδε μὲν Περσῶν τῶν οἰχομένων
Ἑλλάδ᾽ ἐς αἶαν πιστὰ καλεῖται,
καὶ τῶν ἀφνεῶν καὶ πολυχρύσων
ἑδράνων φύλακες, κατὰ πρεσβείαν
οὓς αὐτὸς ἄναξ Ξέρξης βασιλεὺς   5
Δαρειογενὴς
εἵλετο χώρας ἐφορεύειν.
ἀμφὶ δὲ νόστῳ τῷ βασιλείῳ
καὶ πολυχρύσου στρατιᾶς ἤδη
κακόμαντις ἄγαν ὀρσολοπεῖται   10
θυμὸς ἔσωθεν·
πᾶσα γὰρ ἰσχὺς Ἀσιατογενὴς
ᾤχωκε, νέον δ᾽ ἄνδρα βαΰζει,
κοὔτε τις ἄγγελος οὔτε τις ἱππεὺς
ἄστυ τὸ Περσῶν ἀφικνεῖται·   15
οἴτε τὸ Σούσων ἠδ᾽ Ἀγβατάνων
καὶ τὸ παλαιὸν Κίσσιον ἔρκος
προλιπόντες ἔβαν, τοὶ μὲν ἐφ᾽ ἵππων.
τοὶ δ᾽ ἐπὶ ναῶν, πεζοί τε βάδην
πολέμου στῖφος παρέχοντες·   20
οἷος Ἀμίστρης ἠδ᾽ Ἀρταφρένης
καὶ Μεγαβάτης ἠδ᾽ Ἀστάσπης,
ταγοὶ Περσῶν,
βασιλῆς βασιλέως ὕποχοι μεγάλου,
σοῦνται, στρατιᾶς πολλῆς ἔφοροι,   25
τοξοδάμαντές τ᾽ ἠδ᾽ ἱπποβάται,

Persians

[The action takes place in Susa, the capital of the Persian Empire, in front of a large building.]²

[The Chorus enters.]

CHORUS LEADER

    We are here as trustworthy delegates
    for all those Persians who have marched away
    to the land of Greece. Thanks to our old age,
    we are the guardians of the royal home,
    so rich in gold, the men Xerxes himself,
    our king, son of Darius, has chosen
    to supervise his realm. But here inside,
    my heart has for a long time been troubled
    about our golden army's journey home
    and the king's return. It senses trouble.   [10]
    For all the power born out of Asia
    has gone, responding to our young king's call,
    and yet here in the Persians' capital
    no horseman has come back, no courier.
    Streaming out of Susa and Agbatana
    and the ancient parapets of Kissa,
    our forces moved away, some on horseback,
    some by ship, some on foot—a close-packed mass   [20]
    prepared for war—men like Artaphrenes,
    Amistres, Astaspes, and Megabates,
    commanders of Persia's warrior host,
    all kings and yet all ruled by our Great King,
    leaders of a vast army on the march,
    experts in archery and horsemanship,

Aeschylus

φοβεροὶ μὲν ἰδεῖν, δεινοὶ δὲ μάχην
ψυχῆς εὐτλήμονι δόξῃ·
Ἀρτεμβάρης θ᾽ ἱππιοχάρμης
καὶ Μασίστρης, ὅ τε τοξοδάμας   30
ἐσθλὸς Ἰμαῖος, Φαρανδάκης θ᾽,
ἵππων τ᾽ ἐλατὴρ Σοσθάνης.
ἄλλους δ᾽ ὁ μέγας καὶ πολυθρέμμων
Νεῖλος ἔπεμψεν· Σουσισκάνης,
Πηγασταγὼν Αἰγυπτογενής,   35
ὅ τε τῆς ἱερᾶς Μέμφιδος ἄρχων
μέγας Ἀρσάμης, τάς τ᾽ ὠγυγίους
Θήβας ἐφέπων Ἀριόμαρδος,
καὶ ἐλειοβάται ναῶν ἐρέται
δεινοὶ πλῆθός τ᾽ ἀνάριθμοι.   40
ἁβροδιαίτων δ᾽ ἕπεται Λυδῶν
ὄχλος, οἵ τ᾽ ἐπίπαν ἠπειρογενὲς
κατέχουσιν ἔθνος, τοὺς Μητρογαθὴς
Ἀρκτεύς τ᾽ ἀγαθός, βασιλῆς δίοποι,
καὶ πολύχρυσοι Σάρδεις ἐπόχους   45
πολλοῖς ἅρμασιν ἐξορμῶσιν,
δίρρυμά τε καὶ τρίρρυμα τέλη,
φοβερὰν ὄψιν προσιδέσθαι.
στεῦται δ᾽ ἱεροῦ Τμώλου πελάται
ζυγὸν ἀμφιβαλεῖν δούλιον Ἑλλάδι,   50
Μάρδων, Θάρυβις, λόγχης ἄκμονες,
καὶ ἀκοντισταὶ Μυσοί· Βαβυλὼν δ᾽
ἡ πολύχρυσος πάμμικτον ὄχλον
πέμπει σύρδην, ναῶν τ᾽ ἐπόχους
καὶ τοξουλκῷ λήματι πιστούς·   55
τὸ μαχαιροφόρον τ᾽ ἔθνος ἐκ πάσης
Ἀσίας ἕπεται
δειναῖς βασιλέως ὑπὸ πομπαῖς.
τοιόνδ᾽ ἄνθος Περσίδος αἴας
οἴχεται ἀνδρῶν,   60
οὓς πέρι πᾶσα χθὼν Ἀσιῆτις
θρέψασα πόθῳ στένεται μαλερῷ,
τοκέες τ᾽ ἄλοχοί θ᾽ ἡμερολεγδὸν
τείνοντα χρόνον τρομέονται.

6

fearful to look at and terrible in war,
their spirits steeled for battle. With them there
is Artembares the charioteer,   [30]
as well as Masistes, noble Imaeus
so deadly with his bow, Pharandaces,
and Sosthanes, who drives his horses on.
The fertile mighty Nile sent others, too—
Sousiscanes, Egyptian-born Pegastagon,
Arsames, great king of sacred Memphis,
Ariomardos, who rules in ancient Thebes,
and from the marshes men who row the ships,
a frightening horde in countless numbers.

And with them goes a crowd of Lydians,   [40]
luxury loving men, whose force controls
all mainland tribes, warrior ranks sent out
with noble Arcteus and Mitrogathes,
a royal command, and gold-rich Sardis—
huge throngs of chariots streaming out,
row after row of three- and four-horse teams,
a terrifying sight! And men who live
by sacred Tmolus now threaten to hurl   [50]
the yoke of slavery upon the Greeks—
Mardon and Tharybis, with thunderbolts
for spears, and Mysians armed with javelins.³

And Babylon, awash with gold, sends out
huge columns of men of different kinds,
sailors on ships and other troops whose strength
relies on skill in fighting with the bow.
The sabre-bearing races also come
from all of Asia, following the king,
a fearful expedition on the march!
Warriors like these move out, the flower   [60]
of Persian lands, while all of Asia yearns.
Their nurturing mother now longs for them
and groans with fierce desire, as wives and children
count the days and shudder at the long delay.

πεπέρακεν μὲν ὁ περσέπτολις ἤδη 65
βασίλειος στρατὸς εἰς ἀν-
τίπορον γείτονα χώραν,
λινοδέσμῳ σχεδίᾳ πορθ-
μὸν ἀμείψας
Ἀθαμαντίδος Ἕλλας, 70
πολύγομφον ὅδισμα
ζυγὸν ἀμφιβαλὼν αὐχένι πόντου.

πολυάνδρου δ' Ἀσίας θούριος ἄρχων
ἐπὶ πᾶσαν χθόνα ποιμα-
νόριον θεῖον ἐλαύνει 75
διχόθεν, πεζονόμον τ' ἔκ
τε θαλάσσας,
ἐχυροῖσι πεποιθὼς
στυφελοῖς ἐφέταις, χρυ-
σογόνου γενεᾶς ἰσόθεος φώς. 80

κυάνεον δ' ὄμμασι λεύσσων
φονίου δέργμα δράκοντος,
πολύχειρ καὶ πολυναύτας,
Σύριόν θ' ἅρμα διώκων,
ἐπάγει δουρικλύτοις ἀν- 85
δράσι τοξόδαμνον Ἄρη.

δόκιμος δ' οὔτις ὑποστὰς
μεγάλῳ ῥεύματι φωτῶν
ἐχυροῖς ἕρκεσιν εἴργειν
ἄμαχον κῦμα θαλάσσας· 90
ἀπρόσοιστος γὰρ ὁ Περσᾶν
στρατὸς ἀλκίφρων τε λαός.

θεόθεν γὰρ κατὰ Μοῖρ'
ἐκράτησεν τὸ παλαι-
όν, ἐπέσκηψε δὲ Πέρσαις 95
πολέμους πυργοδαΐκτους
διέπειν ἱππιοχάρμας
τε κλόνους
πόλεών τ' ἀναστάσεις.

8

CHORUS

Obliterating cities as it moves,
our royal army has already marched
to neighbouring lands on the facing shore,
crossing the Hellespont, that narrow sea
which gets its name from Athamas' child,
on a floating bridge tied down with cable   [70]
and throwing the yoke of a tight-knit road
across the neck of the sea.4

Through every land
the fiery king of a massive Asian horde
drives on his men—a wondrous warrior pack—
in a double formation by land and sea,
with trust in his brave and stern commanders,
our golden born and godlike king.   [80]

His dark eyes burn
with the glare of a snake aroused to kill.
Soldiers and sailors massing behind him,
he urges his Syrian chariot on,
leading his archers like a war god's host
to fight against men renowned for their spears.

No man has the strength to repel this force,
this irresistible torrent of men,
or with a strong bulwark to hold in check
the overpowering surge of the sea.   [90]
For warriors fill our Persian ranks,
our invincible force of fearless men.

By decrees of the gods since earliest times,
Fate has ruled all and has always ordained
that Persians wage war, knocking down towers,
fighting in chariots, and demolishing cities.

ἔμαθον δ' εὐρυπόροι-   100
ο θαλάσσας πολιαι-
νομένας πνεύματι λάβρῳ
ἐσορᾶν πόντιον ἄλσος,
πίσυνοι λεπτοδόμοις πεί-
σμασι λα-   105
οπόροις τε μαχαναῖς.

δολόμητιν δ' ἀπάταν θεοῦ
τίς ἀνὴρ θνατὸς ἀλύξει;
τίς ὁ κραιπνῷ ποδὶ πήδη-
μα τόδ' εὐπετῶς ἀνάσσων;   110

φιλόφρων γὰρ παρασαίνει
βροτὸν εἰς ἄρκυας Ἄτα,
τόθεν οὐκ ἔστιν ὕπερθέν
νιν ἄνατον ἐξαλύξαι.

ταῦτά μοι μελαγχίτων   115
φρὴν ἀμύσσεται φόβῳ,
ὀᾶ, Περσικοῦ στρατεύματος
τοῦδε, μὴ πόλις πύθη-
ται κένανδρον μέγ' ἄστυ Σουσίδος,

καὶ τὸ Κισσίων πόλισμ'   120
ἀντίδουπον ᾄσεται,
ὀᾶ, τοῦτ' ἔπος γυναικοπλη-
θὴς ὅμιλος ἀπύων,
βυσσίνοις δ' ἐν πέπλοις πέσῃ λακίς.   125

πᾶς γὰρ ἱππηλάτας
καὶ πεδοστιβὴς λεὼς
σμῆνος ὣς ἐκλέλοιπεν μελισ-
σᾶν σὺν ὀρχάμῳ στρατοῦ,
τὸν ἀμφίζευκτον ἐξαμείψας   130
ἀμφοτέρας ἅλιον
πρῶνα κοινὸν αἴας.

10

By trusting their finely made cables and ships
our men have now learned how to gaze on the deep   [100]
when tempestuous storms from the howling winds
whip white surface waters across the broad sea.

But what mortal man can hope to evade
insidious deceit of the gods? What man
with nimble feet can leap above that snare?

For fair Delusion, with her welcoming smile,
spreads her nets wide and lures the man in.
There is no escape—that trap she sets
no man evades by springing back once more.

Such matters hang black thoughts around my heart
and tear at it with fear. Alas for them,
the soldiers of that mighty Persian force!
May our great city Sousa never hear
a cry like that or learn its men have died.

And Kissa's city folk will then all chant   [120]
their own song in reply—Alas! That crowd
of women screaming out will tear apart
their splendid robes of linen.

                    For all our men—
our horse and infantry—like swarms of bees,
have left with the lord who leads our army,
crossing the cape the two continents share,   [130]
now Xerxes has yoked has them together.

Aeschylus

λέκτρα δ' ἀνδρῶν πόθῳ
πίμπλαται δακρύμασιν·
Περσίδες δ' ἁβροπενθεῖς ἑκά-   135
στα πόθῳ φιλάνορι
τὸν αἰχμάεντα θοῦρον εὐνα-
τῆρ' ἀποπεμψαμένα
λείπεται μονόζυξ.

— ἀλλ' ἄγε, Πέρσαι, τόδ' ἐνεζόμενοι   140
στέγος ἀρχαῖον,
φροντίδα κεδνὴν καὶ βαθύβουλον
θώμεθα, χρεία δὲ προσήκει,
πῶς ἄρα πράσσει Ξέρξης βασιλεὺς
Δαρειογενής,   145
τὸ πατρωνύμιον γένος ἡμέτερον·
πότερον τόξου ῥῦμα τὸ νικῶν,
ἢ δορικράνου
λόγχης ἰσχὺς κεκράτηκεν.

ἀλλ' ἥδε θεῶν ἴσον ὀφθαλμοῖς   150
φάος ὁρμᾶται μήτηρ βασιλέως,
βασίλεια δ' ἐμή· προσπίτνω·
καὶ προσφθόγγοις δὲ χρεὼν αὐτὴν
πάντας μύθοισι προσαυδᾶν.

ὦ βαθυζώνων ἄνασσα Περσίδων ὑπερτάτη,   155
μῆτερ ἡ Ξέρξου γεραιά, χαῖρε, Δαρείου γύναι·
θεοῦ μὲν εὐνάτειρα Περσῶν, θεοῦ δὲ καὶ μήτηρ ἔφυς,
εἴ τι μὴ δαίμων παλαιὸς νῦν μεθέστηκε στρατῷ.

ΑΤΟΣΣΑ
ταῦτα δὴ λιποῦσ' ἱκάνω χρυσεοστόλμους δόμους
καὶ τὸ Δαρείου τε κἀμὸν κοινὸν εὐνατήριον.   160
κἀμὲ καρδίαν ἀμύσσει φροντίς· ἐς δ' ὑμᾶς ἐρῶ
μῦθον οὐδαμῶς ἐμαυτῆς οὖσ' ἀδείμαντος, φίλοι,
μὴ μέγας πλοῦτος κονίσας οὖδας ἀντρέψῃ ποδὶ

12

Our marriage beds long for the absent men
and fill with tears, as Persian women grieve,
each one with a woman's heartfelt yearning
for the fearless warrior she sent away.
Her man is gone, and now she sleeps alone.

CHORUS LEADER

Come now, Persians, let us take our seats   [140]
within this ancient place. Let us reflect,
for at this time we need to turn our thoughts
to wise and well-considered counsel
about what is happening with our king,
Xerxes, son of Darius. Have Persian archers
drawn their bows and won, or have the Greeks
with the power of their sharp spears prevailed?

*[Atossa enters with attendants]*⁵

But look—the mother of our king approaches,
like light streaming from the eye of god.
I must prostrate myself before my queen,
and all of you must show her your respect—
salute her majesty with words of welcome.

[The Chorus Leader prostrates himself and speaks to Atossa from his knees.]

Hail to you, O queen, most illustrious
of all deep-waisted Persian women—
Xerxes' aged mother and wife of Darius,
once the consort of Persia's god and now
the mother of their god—unless perhaps
the divinity they used to have of old
has now abandoned Persian warriors.

ATOSSA

That is why I have left my gold-decked home
and the royal bed I shared with Darius   [160]
and have come here. For worries rend my heart.
My friends, I will confide in you—I am afraid
that our vast wealth will quickly stir up dust
and with its foot cast down the great success

ὄλβον, ὃν Δαρεῖος ἦρεν οὐκ ἄνευ θεῶν τινος.

ταῦτά μοι διπλῆ μέριμνα φραστός ἐστιν ἐν φρεσίν, 165
μήτε χρημάτων ἀνάνδρων πλῆθος ἐν τιμῇ σέβειν
μήτ' ἀχρημάτοισι λάμπειν φῶς ὅσον σθένος πάρα.
ἔστι γὰρ πλοῦτός γ' ἀμεμφής, ἀμφὶ δ' ὀφθαλμῷ
φόβος·
ὄμμα γὰρ δόμων νομίζω δεσπότου παρουσίαν.
πρὸς τάδ' ὡς οὕτως ἐχόντων τῶνδε, σύμβουλοι
λόγου 170
τοῦδέ μοι γένεσθε, Πέρσαι, γηραλέα πιστώματα·
πάντα γὰρ τὰ κέδν' ἐν ὑμῖν ἐστί μοι βουλεύματα.

ΧΟΡΟΣ
εὖ τόδ' ἴσθι, γῆς ἄνασσα τῆσδε, μή σε δὶς φράσαι
μήτ' ἔπος μήτ' ἔργον ὧν ἂν δύναμις ἡγεῖσθαι θέλῃ·
εὐμενεῖς γὰρ ὄντας ἡμᾶς τῶνδε συμβούλους καλεῖς. 175

ΑΤΟΣΣΑ
πολλοῖς μὲν αἰεὶ νυκτέροις ὀνείρασιν
ξύνειμ', ἀφ' οὗπερ παῖς ἐμὸς στείλας στρατὸν
Ἰαόνων γῆν οἴχεται πέρσαι θέλων·
ἀλλ' οὔτι πω τοιόνδ' ἐναργὲς εἰδόμην
ὡς τῆς πάροιθεν εὐφρόνης· λέξω δέ σοι. 180
ἐδοξάτην μοι δύο γυναῖκ' εὐείμονε,
ἡ μὲν πέπλοισι Περσικοῖς ἠσκημένη,
ἡ δ' αὖτε Δωρικοῖσιν, εἰς ὄψιν μολεῖν,
μεγέθει τε τῶν νῦν ἐκπρεπεστάτα πολύ,
κάλλει τ' ἀμώμω, καὶ κασιγνήτα γένους 185
ταὐτοῦ· πάτραν δ' ἔναιον ἡ μὲν Ἑλλάδα
κλήρῳ λαχοῦσα γαῖαν, ἡ δὲ βάρβαρον.
τούτω στάσιν τιν', ὡς ἐγὼ 'δόκουν ὁρᾶν,
τεύχειν ἐν ἀλλήλαισι· παῖς δ' ἐμὸς μαθὼν

14

which—thanks to the assistance of some god—
king Darius achieved. And that is why
my mind is burdened with a double care,
which I find difficult to speak about.
The common folk do not respect great wealth
unless backed up with men, and though the poor
may have great strength, the light of their success
will never shine. Now, we have wealth enough,
but still I fear for what I hold to be
our finest treasure, true riches in the home,
the lord and master's eye. Since that is so,   [170]
Persians, you old trustworthy counsellors,
advise me what to do, since all my hopes
for level-headed guidance rest on you.

CHORUS LEADER
You are our country's queen—so rest assured
you do not need to ask us twice for help,
for anything that lies with our power
to say or do. You have summoned us here
as counsellors in this affair, and we
are well disposed to serve your interests.

ATOSSA
Many dreams keep visiting me at night—
all the time—ever since my son prepared
his army and set off, hoping to destroy
Ionian lands. But this past night
I had one more distinct than all the rest.
I will describe it to you. I seemed to see   [180]
two women dressed in very lovely clothes—
one wore Persian robes, the other Dorian.[6]
They came in view—both of gigantic size,
much larger than the women of today,
and very beautiful. They were sisters,
of the same family line. One of them
lived in Hellenic lands, assigned by lot,
the other dwelt among barbarians.[7]
And as I watched, I seemed to see these two
begin to fight each other. Then my son,

15

Aeschylus

κατεῖχε κἀπράυνεν, ἅρμασιν δ' ὕπο   190
ζεύγνυσιν αὐτὼ καὶ λέπαδν' ἐπ' αὐχένων
τίθησι. χὴ μὲν τῇδ' ἐπυργοῦτο στολῇ
ἐν ἡνίαισί τ' εἶχεν εὔαρκτον στόμα,
ἡ δ' ἐσφάδαζε, καὶ χεροῖν ἔντη δίφρου
διασπαράσσει καὶ ξυναρπάζει βίᾳ   195
ἄνευ χαλινῶν καὶ ζυγὸν θραύει μέσον.
πίπτει δ' ἐμὸς παῖς, καὶ πατὴρ παρίσταται
Δαρεῖος οἰκτείρων σφε· τὸν δ' ὅπως ὁρᾷ
Ξέρξης, πέπλους ῥήγνυσιν ἀμφὶ σώματι.
καὶ ταῦτα μὲν δὴ νυκτὸς εἰσιδεῖν λέγω.   200
ἐπεὶ δ' ἀνέστην καὶ χεροῖν καλλιρρόου
ἔψαυσα πηγῆς, σὺν θυηπόλῳ χερὶ
βωμὸν προσέστην, ἀποτρόποισι δαίμοσιν
θέλουσα θῦσαι πέλανον, ὧν τέλη τάδε.
ὁρῶ δὲ φεύγοντ' αἰετὸν πρὸς ἐσχάραν   205
Φοίβου· φόβῳ δ' ἄφθογγος ἐστάθην, φίλοι·
μεθύστερον δὲ κίρκον εἰσορῶ δρόμῳ
πτεροῖς ἐφορμαίνοντα καὶ χηλαῖς κάρα
τίλλονθ'· ὁ δ' οὐδὲν ἄλλο γ' ἢ πτήξας δέμας
παρεῖχε. ταῦτ' ἔμοιγε δείματ' εἰσιδεῖν,   210
ὑμῖν δ' ἀκούειν. εὖ γὰρ ἴστε, παῖς ἐμὸς
πράξας μὲν εὖ θαυμαστὸς ἂν γένοιτ' ἀνήρ,
κακῶς δὲ πράξας, οὐχ ὑπεύθυνος πόλει,
σωθεὶς δ' ὁμοίως τῆσδε κοιρανεῖ χθονός.

ΧΟΡΟΣ

οὔ σε βουλόμεσθα, μῆτερ, οὔτ' ἄγαν φοβεῖν λόγοις   215
οὔτε θαρσύνειν. θεοὺς δὲ προστροπαῖς ἱκνουμένη,

16

once he learned of this, tried to hold them back
and calm them down. Around their necks he set   [190]
a collar strap and yoked it to his chariot.
One sister carried her restraint with pride
and kept her mouth compliant in the reins.
The other one fought back—her hands tore at
the chariot harness and, freed from her restraint,
dragged it so hard she broke the yoke in two.
My son fell out headfirst, and Darius,
his father, who stood close by, was grieving.
Then Xerxes, when he saw his father there,
shred the garments covering his body.
That was the dream I saw during the night.   [200]
When I got up, I went to wash my hands
in a flowing spring, and holding up a gift,
I stood beside an altar, intending
to offer sacrifice to those deities
who ward off evil, with those rituals
which are their due. But then I saw an eagle
swooping down for safety at the altar
of Apollo, and I was terrified.
My friends, as I stood there speechless, I saw
a hawk racing up behind, wings outspread.
Its talons clawed and ripped the eagle's head.
The eagle did not fight but cowered down
and left its body open to attack.
Seeing this visions made me so afraid—   [210]
and hearing them you must be fearful, too.
For you know well that if my son succeeds
he will become a man men hold in awe,
but even if he fails, those in the city
cannot hold him accountable, for Xerxes,
if he gets safely back, still rules this land.

CHORUS LEADER

Lady mother, we do not wish our words
to make you fearful or offer you false hope.
But if what you have seen is ominous,
approach the gods with prayers, begging them

17

Aeschylus

εἴ τι φλαῦρον εἶδες, αἰτοῦ τῶνδ᾽ ἀποτροπὴν τελεῖν,

τὰ δ᾽ ἀγάθ᾽ ἐκτελῆ γενέσθαι σοί τε καὶ τέκνοις σέθεν

καὶ πόλει φίλοις τε πᾶσι. δεύτερον δὲ χρὴ χοὰς

Γῆ τε καὶ φθιτοῖς χέασθαι· πρευμενῶς δ᾽ αἰτοῦ τάδε,   220

σὸν πόσιν Δαρεῖον, ὅνπερ φὴς ἰδεῖν κατ᾽ εὐφρόνην,

ἐσθλά σοι πέμπειν τέκνῳ τε γῆς ἔνερθεν ἐς φάος,

τἄμπαλιν δὲ τῶνδε γαίᾳ κάτοχα μαυροῦσθαι σκότῳ.

ταῦτα θυμόμαντις ὢν σοι πρευμενῶς παρήνεσα.

εὖ δὲ πανταχῇ τελεῖν σοι τῶνδε κρίνομεν πέρι.   225

ΑΤΟΣΣΑ

ἀλλὰ μὴν εὔνους γ᾽ ὁ πρῶτος τῶνδ᾽ ἐνυπνίων κριτὴς

παιδὶ καὶ δόμοις ἐμοῖσι τήνδ᾽ ἐκύρωσας φάτιν.

ἐκτελοῖτο δὴ τὰ χρηστά· ταῦτα δ᾽, ὡς ἐφίεσαι,

πάντα θήσομεν θεοῖσι τοῖς τ᾽ ἔνερθε γῆς φίλοις,

εὖτ᾽ ἂν εἰς οἴκους μόλωμεν. κεῖνα δ᾽ ἐκμαθεῖν θέλω,   230

ὦ φίλοι, ποῦ τὰς Ἀθήνας φασὶν ἱδρῦσθαι χθονός.

ΧΟΡΟΣ

τῆλε πρὸς δυσμαῖς ἄνακτος Ἡλίου φθινασμάτων.

ΑΤΟΣΣΑ

ἀλλὰ μὴν ἵμειρ᾽ ἐμὸς παῖς τήνδε θηρᾶσαι πόλιν;

ΧΟΡΟΣ

πᾶσα γὰρ γένοιτ᾽ ἂν Ἑλλὰς βασιλέως ὑπήκοος.

18

to avert the evil and bring about
what is of benefit to you, your sons,
the city, all your family and friends.
Then you must pour libations to the earth
and to the dead, and with auspicious words   [220]
ask Darius, your husband, whom you say
you saw last night, to confer his blessing
from underneath the earth up to the light,
on you and on your son, and to hold down
what works against you and keep it buried
deep within the earth, hidden in the dark.
From what I understand of prophecy
and as a friend I give you this advice.
I sense that in these matters everything
will turn out favourably for you.

ATOSSA

You are the first one who has offered me
an interpretation of the dreams I had,
and you have clearly shown in what you say
your kindness to my child and family.
May things all turn out well! When I return
back to the palace, I will carry out
those rituals for the gods and loved ones
underneath the earth, the way you have advised.
But, friends, there is one thing I wish to know.   [230]
In what part of the world do people say
this city of Athens is located?

CHORUS LEADER

Far away from here, where our Lord the Sun
grows dim and sets.

ATOSSA

                                And is it really true
my son desired to conquer such a place?

CHORUS LEADER

Yes, he did. For then all lands in Hellas
would be subject to our King.

Aeschylus

ΑΤΟΣΣΑ

ὧδέ τις πάρεστιν αὐτοῖς ἀνδροπλήθεια στρατοῦ;   235

ΧΟΡΟΣ

καὶ στρατὸς τοιοῦτος, ἔρξας πολλὰ δὴ Μήδους κακά.

ΑΤΟΣΣΑ

καὶ τί πρὸς τούτοισιν ἄλλο; πλοῦτος ἐξαρκὴς δόμοις;

ΧΟΡΟΣ

ἀργύρου πηγή τις αὐτοῖς ἐστι, θησαυρὸς χθονός.

ΑΤΟΣΣΑ

πότερα γὰρ τοξουλκὸς αἰχμὴ διὰ χεροῖν αὐτοῖς πρέπει;

ΧΟΡΟΣ

οὐδαμῶς· ἔγχη σταδαῖα καὶ φεράσπιδες σαγαί.   240

ΑΤΟΣΣΑ

τίς δὲ ποιμάνωρ ἔπεστι κἀπιδεσπόζει στρατῷ;

ΧΟΡΟΣ

οὔτινος δοῦλοι κέκληνται φωτὸς οὐδ᾽ ὑπήκοοι.

ΑΤΟΣΣΑ

πῶς ἂν οὖν μένοιεν ἄνδρας πολεμίους ἐπήλυδας;

ΧΟΡΟΣ

ὥστε Δαρείου πολύν τε καὶ καλὸν φθεῖραι στρατόν.

ΑΤΟΣΣΑ

δεινά τοι λέγεις ἰόντων τοῖς τεκοῦσι φροντίσαι.   245

20

ATOSSA

          And these Greeks—
does their army consist of many men?

CHORUS LEADER

    Their army has been strong enough before
to have done much damage to the Medes.[8]

ATOSSA

    Are their hands trained to fight with well-strung bows?

CHORUS LEADER

    No, not at all—they arm themselves with shields
and fight in close with spears.

ATOSSA

                What other things
do they possess? Do they have wealth at home—
all the money they need?

CHORUS LEADER

              They have a mine,
a fountain of silver—their country's treasure.[9]   [240]

ATOSSA

    Who governs them? Who commands their army?

CHORUS LEADER

    People say they are no man's slaves or servants.

ATOSSA

    Then how can they turn back a fierce attack
when warlike men invade?

CHORUS LEADER

           Well, they managed
to destroy that great and glorious force
which Darius had sent against them.

ATOSSA

    For those whose sons have left, those words of yours
are ominous to think of.

ΧΟΡΟΣ

ἀλλ' ἐμοὶ δοκεῖν τάχ' εἴσῃ πάντα νημερτῆ λόγον.
τοῦδε γὰρ δράμημα φωτὸς Περσικὸν πρέπει μαθεῖν,
καὶ φέρει σαφές τι πρᾶγος ἐσθλὸν ἢ κακὸν κλύειν.

ΑΓΓΕΛΟΣ

ὦ γῆς ἁπάσης Ἀσιάδος πολίσματα,
ὦ Περσὶς αἶα καὶ πολὺς πλούτου λιμήν,   250
ὡς ἐν μιᾷ πληγῇ κατέφθαρται πολὺς
ὄλβος, τὸ Περσῶν δ' ἄνθος οἴχεται πεσόν.
ὤμοι, κακὸν μὲν πρῶτον ἀγγέλλειν κακά·
ὅμως δ' ἀνάγκη πᾶν ἀναπτύξαι πάθος,
Πέρσαι· στρατὸς γὰρ πᾶς ὄλωλε βαρβάρων.   255

ΧΟΡΟΣ

ἄνι' ἄνια κακὰ
νεόκοτα καὶ δάι'. αἰαῖ,
διαίνεσθε, Πέρσαι,
τόδ' ἄχος κλύοντες.

ΑΓΓΕΛΟΣ

ὡς πάντα γ' ἔστ' ἐκεῖνα διαπεπραγμένα·   260
αὐτὸς δ' ἀέλπτως νόστιμον βλέπω φάος.

ΧΟΡΟΣ

ἦ μακροβίοτος
ὅδε γέ τις αἰὼν ἐφάνθη
γεραιοῖς, ἀκούειν
τόδε πῆμ' ἄελπτον.   265

ΑΓΓΕΛΟΣ

καὶ μὴν παρών γε κοὐ λόγους ἄλλων κλύων,
Πέρσαι, φράσαιμ' ἂν οἷ' ἐπορσύνθη κακά.

22

CHORUS LEADER

> It seems to me
> you will soon know the truth of what's gone on.
> Why else would a Persian man be rushing here.
> He must be bringing news of some event—
> it's clearly something good or bad.

[Enter the Messenger, in great haste. He falls prostrate before Atossa and delivers his first speeches from his knees]

MESSENGER

> O you cities throughout all Asian lands,
> O realm of Persia, haven of vast wealth,   [250]
> one blow has smashed your great prosperity—
> the flower of Persia has been destroyed!
> Our men have perished! Alas! It's terrible
> to be first to tell disastrous news,
> and yet, you Persians, I must now provide
> a full report of that catastrophe—
> our whole barbarian army has been killed!

CHORUS

> Such dreadful, dreadful news!
> So cruel and unforeseen.
> Alas! Alas! Weep now,
> you Persians, as you learn
> of this calamity!

MESSENGER

> Yes, weep, for all those men have been wiped out,   [260]
> while I look on this unexpected day
> when I have come back home.

CHORUS

> For older men, this life of ours
> has been too long, it seems—
> we have to learn about
> this unanticipated grief.

MESSENGER

> I was there—I did not hear what happened
> from other men—so, Persians, I can speak
> directly of the evil things we faced.

23

Aeschylus

ΧΟΡΟΣ
ὀτοτοτοῖ, μάταν
τὰ πολλὰ βέλεα παμμιγῆ
γᾶς ἀπ' Ἀσίδος ἦλθε δᾴ-   270
αν ἐφ' Ἑλλάδα χώραν.

ΑΓΓΕΛΟΣ
πλήθουσι νεκρῶν δυσπότμως ἐφθαρμένων
Σαλαμῖνος ἀκταὶ πᾶς τε πρόσχωρος τόπος.

ΧΟΡΟΣ
ὀτοτοτοῖ, φίλων
ἁλίδονα μέλεα πολυβαφῆ   275
κατθανόντα λέγεις φέρε-
σθαι πλάγκτ' ἐν διπλάκεσσιν.

ΑΓΓΕΛΟΣ
οὐδὲν γὰρ ἤρκει τόξα, πᾶς δ' ἀπώλλυτο
στρατὸς δαμασθεὶς ναΐοισιν ἐμβολαῖς

ΧΟΡΟΣ
ἴυζ' ἄποτμον Πέρσαις   280
δυσαιανῆ βοὰν
δᾴοις, ὡς πάντα παγκάκως
ἔφθισαν· αἰαῖ στρατοῦ φθαρέντος.

ΑΓΓΕΛΟΣ
ὦ πλεῖστον ἔχθος ὄνομα Σαλαμῖνος κλύειν.
φεῦ, τῶν Ἀθηνῶν ὡς στένω μεμνημένος.   285

ΧΟΡΟΣ
στυγναί γ' Ἀθᾶναι δᾴοις·
μεμνῆσθαί τοι πάρα
ὡς πολλὰς Περσίδων μάταν
ἔκτισαν εὔνιδας ἠδ' ἀνάνδρους.

24

CHORUS

    Aaaiii! Our great host
    with all its different weapons
    set out from Asian lands in vain   [270]
    to the mighty land of Hellas!

MESSENGER

    The corpses fill the shores of Salamis
    and all the coasts nearby—our wretched dead.[10]

CHORUS

    Alas! Such grief! You say
    the bodies of the ones we love
    are tossing in the surf,
    being driven back and forth
    and carried by the shifting waves.

MESSENGER

    Our bows were no defence. Our men perished.
    The entire force was overwhelmed at sea
    when Ionian ships attacked our fleet.

CHORUS

    Cry a sorrowful lament,   [280]
    a pitiful dirge for our dead,
    those ill-starred Persian men!
    The gods bring all this evil!
    Aaaaiii! Aaaiii!
    The army is now gone!

MESSENGER

    That name Salamis—a hateful word,
    the most offensive to my ears. Alas,
    how I groan when I remember Athens!

CHORUS

    Yes, Athens is hateful to her foes!
    We well recall how Athens made
    so many Persian women widows
    by slaughtering their men.[11]

ΑΤΟΣΣΑ

σιγῶ πάλαι δύστηνος ἐκπεπληγμένη   290
κακοῖς· ὑπερβάλλει γὰρ ἥδε συμφορὰ
τὸ μήτε λέξαι μήτ' ἐρωτῆσαι πάθη.

ὅμως δ' ἀνάγκη πημονὰς βροτοῖς φέρειν
θεῶν διδόντων· πᾶν δ' ἀναπτύξας πάθος
λέξον καταστάς, κεἰ στένεις κακοῖς ὅμως.   295
τίς οὐ τέθνηκε, τίνα δὲ καὶ πενθήσομεν
τῶν ἀρχελείων, ὅστ' ἐπὶ σκηπτουχίᾳ
ταχθεὶς ἄνανδρον τάξιν ἠρήμου θανών;

ΑΓΓΕΛΟΣ

Ξέρξης μὲν αὐτὸς ζῇ τε καὶ βλέπει φάος.

ΑΤΟΣΣΑ

ἐμοῖς μὲν εἶπας δώμασιν φάος μέγα   300
καὶ λευκὸν ἦμαρ νυκτὸς ἐκ μελαγχίμου.

ΑΓΓΕΛΟΣ

Ἀρτεμβάρης δὲ μυρίας ἵππου βραβεὺς
στύφλους παρ' ἀκτὰς θείνεται Σιληνιῶν.
χὠ χιλίαρχος Δαδάκης πληγῇ δορὸς
πήδημα κοῦφον ἐκ νεὼς ἀφήλατο·   305
Τενάγων τ' ἀριστεὺς Βακτρίων ἰθαιγενὴς
θαλασσόπληκτον νῆσον Αἴαντος πολεῖ.
Λίλαιος, Ἀρσάμης τε κἀργήστης τρίτος,
οἵδ' ἀμφὶ νῆσον τὴν πελειοθρέμμονα
δινούμενοι 'κύρισσον ἰσχυρὰν χθόνα·   310
πηγαῖς τε Νείλου γειτονῶν Αἰγυπτίου

26

ATOSSA

> I have kept quiet for a long time here, [290]
> struck silent by the news of this defeat.
> For this event is too calamitous
> to talk or even ask about the pain.
> Yet suffering is something mortal beings
> must learn to bear when it comes from the gods.
> So stand up now and speak. Give your report—
> and even if you groan at this bad news,
> describe the full extent of our defeat.
> Who did not die? What about the leaders?
> Which ones should we mourn? And of all those men
> appointed to a sceptre-bearing post,
> which ones have died and left a vacancy
> among the ranks of our commanders?

[The Messenger stands up]

MESSENGER

> Xerxes himself survived—he is alive
> and sees the light of day.

ATOSSA

>   What you have said
> brings a great light of hope into my home, [300]
> a bright dawn after grim black drapes of night.

MESSENGER

> But Artembares, who led ten thousand horse,
> is being smashed against the cruel shores
> of Salamis, and Dadaces, who led
> a thousand men, was hit by a spear
> and with an easy leap fell from his ship.
> Tenagon, the finest of that ancient race
> from Bactria, now moves around the isle
> of Ajax, a coastline pounded by the sea.[12]
> Lilaios, Arsames, and a third one,
> Argestes are washed around that island,
> a breeding place for doves, as they are thrown
> against its rugged shore. Of all those men [310]
> living beside the springs of Egypt's Nile,

27

Aeschylus

Ἀρκτεύς, Ἀδεύης, καὶ φερεσσάκης τρίτος
Φαρνοῦχος, οἵδε ναὸς ἐκ μιᾶς πέσον.
Χρυσεὺς Μάταλλος μυριόνταρχος θανών,
ἵππου μελαίνης ἡγεμὼν τρισμυρίας,   315
πυρρὰν ζαπληθῆ δάσκιον γενειάδα
ἔτεγγ᾽, ἀμείβων χρῶτα πορφυρέᾳ βαφῇ.
καὶ Μᾶγος Ἄραβος, Ἀρτάβης τε Βάκτριος,
σκληρᾶς μέτοικος γῆς, ἐκεῖ κατέφθιτο.
Ἄμιστρις Ἀμφιστρεύς τε πολύπονον δόρυ   320
νωμῶν, ὅ τ᾽ ἐσθλὸς Ἀριόμαρδος Σάρδεσι
πένθος παρασχών, Σεισάμης θ᾽ ὁ Μύσιος,
Θάρυβίς τε πεντήκοντα πεντάκις νεῶν
ταγός, γένος Λυρναῖος, εὐειδὴς ἀνήρ,
κεῖται θανὼν δείλαιος οὐ μάλ᾽ εὐτυχῶς·   325
Συέννεσίς τε πρῶτος εἰς εὐψυχίαν,
Κιλίκων ἄπαρχος, εἷς ἀνὴρ πλεῖστον πόνον
ἐχθροῖς παρασχών εὐκλεῶς ἀπώλετο.
τοσόνδε ταγῶν νῦν ὑπεμνήσθην πέρι.
πολλῶν παρόντων δ᾽ ὀλίγ᾽ ἀπαγγέλλω κακά.   330

ΑΤΟΣΣΑ

αἰαῖ, κακῶν ὕψιστα δὴ κλύω τάδε,
αἴσχη τε Πέρσαις καὶ λιγέα κωκύματα.
ἀτὰρ φράσον μοι τοῦτ᾽ ἀναστρέψας πάλιν·
πόσον δὲ πλῆθος ἦν νεῶν Ἑλληνίδων,
ὥστ᾽ ἀξιῶσαι Περσικῷ στρατεύματι   335
μάχην συνάψαι ναΐοισιν ἐμβολαῖς;

ΑΓΓΕΛΟΣ

πλήθους μὲν ἂν σάφ᾽ ἴσθ᾽ ἔκατι βάρβαρον
ναυσὶν κρατῆσαι. καὶ γὰρ Ἕλλησιν μὲν ἦν
ὁ πᾶς ἀριθμὸς ἐς τριακάδας δέκα
ναῶν, δεκὰς δ᾽ ἦν τῶνδε χωρὶς ἔκκριτος·   340
Ξέρξῃ δέ, καὶ γὰρ οἶδα, χιλιὰς μὲν ἦν

28

Pharnouchos fell, and three men from one ship,
Pheresseues and Adeues
and Arcteus. And Matallos from Chryse,
who ruled an army of ten thousand men,
as he died, stained his thick, dark, shaggy beard
and changed its colour with a blood-red dye.
Arabos the Magian perished there,
and so did Artabes from Bactria,
who led black horsemen thirty thousand strong
and now has settled deep in rocky ground,
as well as Amistris and Amphistreus,   [320]
who held a deadly spear, and Ariomardus,
a noble man whose death makes Sardis grieve,
and Seisames from Mysia. Tharybis,
commander of two hundred fifty ships,
a handsome man, by birth a Lyrnaean,
now lies in miserable death—his luck
abandoned him. And Suennesis, too,
who ruled Cilicians and by himself
brought so much suffering to his enemies,
for of courageous men he was the best,
fought valiantly and died. I have listed
these men by name, but we lost so many!
What I have told you mentions just a few.   [330]

ATOSSA

Alas! Alas! I have listened to your words,
the height of our misfortune—a disgrace
to Persia, cause enough for screams of grief.
But return to your report and tell me this—
What was the number of the Grecian fleet?
What made them confident enough
to risk a fight at sea with Persian ships?

MESSENGER

You can be sure that we barbarians
would have overwhelmed their fleet, if numbers
had been the only thing. For the Greeks had,
in total, three hundred ships. Ten of these   [340]
were chosen as a special group. But Xerxes—
I can confirm this—led a thousand ships,

Aeschylus

ὧν ἦγε πλῆθος, αἱ δ' ὑπέρκοποι τάχει
ἑκατὸν δὶς ἦσαν ἑπτά θ'· ὧδ' ἔχει λόγος.
μή σοι δοκοῦμεν τῇδε λειφθῆναι μάχῃ;
ἀλλ' ὧδε δαίμων τις κατέφθειρε στρατόν,   345
τάλαντα βρίσας οὐκ ἰσορρόπῳ τύχῃ.
θεοὶ πόλιν σῴζουσι Παλλάδος θεᾶς.

ΑΤΟΣΣΑ
ἔτ' ἄρ' Ἀθηνῶν ἔστ' ἀπόρθητος πόλις;

ΑΓΓΕΛΟΣ
ἀνδρῶν γὰρ ὄντων ἕρκος ἐστὶν ἀσφαλές.

ΑΤΟΣΣΑ
ἀρχὴ δὲ ναυσὶ συμβολῆς τίς ἦν, φράσον·   350
τίνες κατῆρξαν, πότερον Ἕλληνες, μάχης,
ἢ παῖς ἐμός, πλήθει καταυχήσας νεῶν;

ΑΓΓΕΛΟΣ
ἦρξεν μέν, ὦ δέσποινα, τοῦ παντὸς κακοῦ
φανεὶς ἀλάστωρ ἢ κακὸς δαίμων ποθέν.
ἀνὴρ γὰρ Ἕλλην ἐξ Ἀθηναίων στρατοῦ   355
ἐλθὼν ἔλεξε παιδὶ σῷ Ξέρξῃ τάδε,
ὡς εἰ μελαίνης νυκτὸς ἵξεται κνέφας,
Ἕλληνες οὐ μενοῖεν, ἀλλὰ σέλμασιν
ναῶν ἐπανθορόντες ἄλλος ἄλλοσε
δρασμῷ κρυφαίῳ βίοτον ἐκσωσοίατο.   360
ὁ δ' εὐθὺς ὡς ἤκουσεν, οὐ ξυνεὶς δόλον
Ἕλληνος ἀνδρὸς οὐδὲ τὸν θεῶν φθόνον,
πᾶσιν προφωνεῖ τόνδε ναυάρχοις λόγον,

«εὖτ' ἂν φλέγων ἀκτῖσιν ἥλιος χθόνα
λήξῃ, κνέφας δὲ τέμενος αἰθέρος λάβῃ,   365
τάξαι νεῶν στῖφος μὲν ἐν στοίχοις τρισὶν
ἔκπλους φυλάσσειν καὶ πόρους ἁλιρρόθους,

two hundred and seven of which could sail
extremely fast. That's how the numbers stood.
Surely you cannot think that when we fought
we were outnumbered? No. Some deity
did not weigh the scales of fortune fairly
and destroyed our fleet. The gods protect
that city of the goddess Pallas.

ATOSSA

And so,
the city of Athens remains unscathed.[13]

MESSENGER

Yes. While its citizens are still alive
it has a fortress that will never fail.

ATOSSA

Tell me how the battle with the ships began.   [350]
Who was the first to fight? Was it the Greeks?
Or was my son happy to engage their fleet,
given the huge number of his ships?

MESSENGER

My queen, a demon or evil spirit
appeared from somewhere and set in motion
everything that led to our complete collapse.
A man from the Athenian forces,
a Greek, came to Xerxes, your son, and said
that after night arrived and it grew dark
the Greeks would not remain where they were now,
but leap onto the benches in their ships
and, by moving stealthily here and there,
would try to row away and save their lives.   [360]
Xerxes did not sense the Greek man's cunning
or the envy of the gods.[14] So once he heard
what the man had said, he quickly issued
the following orders to his captains:

"When the sun's rays no longer warm the earth
and darkness seizes regions of the sky,
draw up the ships into a triple line
and block the exits to the roaring sea.

ἄλλας δὲ κύκλῳ νῆσον Αἴαντος πέριξ·
ὡς εἰ μόρον φευξοίαθ᾿ Ἕλληνες κακόν,
ναυσὶν κρυφαίως δρασμὸν εὑρόντες τινά, 370
πᾶσιν στέρεσθαι κρατὸς ἦν προκείμενον.»

τοσαῦτ᾿ ἔλεξε κἄρθ᾿ ὑπ᾿ εὐθύμου φρενός·
οὐ γὰρ τὸ μέλλον ἐκ θεῶν ἠπίστατο.
οἱ δ᾿ οὐκ ἀκόσμως, ἀλλὰ πειθάρχῳ φρενὶ
δεῖπνόν τ᾿ ἐπορσύνοντο, ναυβάτης τ᾿ ἀνὴρ 375
τροποῦτο κώπην σκαλμὸν ἀμφ᾿ εὐήρετμον.
ἐπεὶ δὲ φέγγος ἡλίου κατέφθιτο
καὶ νὺξ ἐπῄει, πᾶς ἀνὴρ κώπης ἄναξ
ἐς ναῦν ἐχώρει πᾶς θ᾿ ὅπλων ἐπιστάτης·
τάξις δὲ τάξιν παρεκάλει νεὼς μακρᾶς· 380
πλέουσι δ᾿ ὡς ἕκαστος ἦν τεταγμένος,
καὶ πάννυχοι δὴ διάπλοον καθίστασαν
ναῶν ἄνακτες πάντα ναυτικὸν λεών.
καὶ νὺξ ἐχώρει, κοὐ μάλ᾿ Ἑλλήνων στρατὸς
κρυφαῖον ἔκπλουν οὐδαμῇ καθίστατο· 385
ἐπεί γε μέντοι λευκόπωλος ἡμέρα
πᾶσαν κατέσχε γαῖαν εὐφεγγὴς ἰδεῖν,
πρῶτον μὲν ἠχῇ κέλαδος Ἑλλήνων πάρα
μολπηδὸν ηὐφήμησεν, ὄρθιον δ᾿ ἅμα
ἀντηλάλαξε νησιώτιδος πέτρας 390
ἠχώ· φόβος δὲ πᾶσι βαρβάροις παρῆν
γνώμης ἀποσφαλεῖσιν· οὐ γὰρ ὡς φυγῇ
παιᾶν᾿ ἐφύμνουν σεμνὸν Ἕλληνες τότε,
ἀλλ᾿ ἐς μάχην ὁρμῶντες εὐψύχῳ θράσει·
σάλπιγξ δ᾿ ἀϋτῇ πάντ᾿ ἐκεῖν᾿ ἐπέφλεγεν. 395
εὐθὺς δὲ κώπης ῥοθιάδος ξυνεμβολῇ
ἔπαισαν ἅλμην βρύχιον ἐκ κελεύματος,
θοῶς δὲ πάντες ἦσαν ἐκφανεῖς ἰδεῖν.
τὸ δεξιὸν μὲν πρῶτον εὐτάκτως κέρας
ἡγεῖτο κόσμῳ, δεύτερον δ᾿ ὁ πᾶς στόλος 400

32

With other vessels form a tight blockade
around that isle of Ajax. If the Greeks
escape their evil fate and somehow find
a secret way to steal off in their ships,   [370]
my orders are that all will lose their heads."

When Xerxes said these words, his heart and mind
were fully confident—he had no inkling
of what the gods had planned. His men obeyed.
Their spirits showed no lack of discipline,
as they prepared a meal and every sailor
lashed his oar in place against the thole pin.
Once the sun's light had disappeared and night
came creeping in, each master of his oar
and all the soldiers under arms went down
into the ships, and as the long boats sailed
to take up their assigned positions, row by row,
the men called out to cheer each other on.   [380]
So all night long the officers and crews
kept sailing back and forth on their patrol,
yet as night passed, the Greek force did not try
to slip away in secret. But when the day
rode up with her white steeds and radiant light
seized all the earth, at first we heard a shout.
A resounding cry came from the Greeks—
it sounded like a song—and right away
the echo brought a clarion response
reverberating from the island rocks.   [390]
Then panic struck the whole barbarian fleet.
Our plan had failed, for at that point the Greeks
did not call out their solemn holy cry
as if they meant to flee. No. They sounded
like men who meant to fight with courage
in their hearts. And when a trumpet pealed,
they all caught fire. Then, once the order came,
with one united sweep their foaming oars
struck the salty sea, and their fleet of ships
quickly came in sight, all clearly visible.
First of all, their well organized right wing
advanced in order. Then the entire force   [400]

33

ἐπεξεχώρει, καὶ παρῆν ὁμοῦ κλύειν
πολλὴν βοήν, "ὦ παῖδες Ἑλλήνων ἴτε,
ἐλευθεροῦτε πατρίδ᾽, ἐλευθεροῦτε δὲ
παῖδας, γυναῖκας, θεῶν τέ πατρῴων ἕδη,
θήκας τε προγόνων· νῦν ὑπὲρ πάντων ἀγών." 405
καὶ μὴν παρ᾽ ἡμῶν Περσίδος γλώσσης ῥόθος
ὑπηντίαζε, κοὐκέτ᾽ ἦν μέλλειν ἀκμή.
εὐθὺς δὲ ναῦς ἐν νηὶ χαλκήρη στόλον
ἔπαισεν· ἦρξε δ᾽ ἐμβολῆς Ἑλληνικὴ
ναῦς, κἀποθραύει πάντα Φοινίσσης νεὼς 410
κόρυμβ᾽, ἐπ᾽ ἄλλην δ᾽ ἄλλος ηὔθυνεν δόρυ.
τὰ πρῶτα μέν νυν ῥεῦμα Περσικοῦ στρατοῦ
ἀντεῖχεν· ὡς δὲ πλῆθος ἐν στενῷ νεῶν
ἤθροιστ᾽ ἀρωγὴ δ᾽ οὔτις ἀλλήλοις παρῆν,
αὐτοὶ δ᾽ ὑφ᾽ αὑτῶν ἐμβόλοις χαλκοστόμοις 415
παίοντ᾽, ἔθραυον πάντα κωπήρη στόλον,
Ἑλληνικαί τε νῆες οὐκ ἀφρασμόνως
κύκλῳ πέριξ ἔθεινον, ὑπτιοῦτο δὲ
σκάφη νεῶν, θάλασσα δ᾽ οὐκέτ᾽ ἦν ἰδεῖν,
ναυαγίων πλήθουσα καὶ φόνου βροτῶν. 420
ἀκταὶ δὲ νεκρῶν χοιράδες τ᾽ ἐπλήθυον,
φυγῇ δ᾽ ἀκόσμῳ πᾶσα ναῦς ἠρέσσετο,
ὅσαιπερ ἦσαν βαρβάρου στρατεύματος.
τοὶ δ᾽ ὥστε θύννους ἤ τιν᾽ ἰχθύων βόλον
ἀγαῖσι κωπῶν θραύμασίν τ᾽ ἐρειπίων 425
ἔπαιον, ἐρράχιζον· οἰμωγὴ δ᾽ ὁμοῦ
κωκύμασιν κατεῖχε πελαγίαν ἅλα,
ἕως κελαινῆς νυκτὸς ὄμμ᾽ ἀφείλετο.
κακῶν δὲ πλῆθος, οὐδ᾽ ἂν εἰ δέκ᾽ ἤματα
στοιχηγοροίην, οὐκ ἂν ἐκπλήσαιμί σοι. 430
εὖ γὰρ τόδ᾽ ἴσθι, μηδάμ᾽ ἡμέρα μιᾷ
πλῆθος τοσουτάριθμον ἀνθρώπων θανεῖν.

moved up, and, as it did, we all could hear
a mighty cry:

             "You offspring of the Greeks,
come on! Free your native home! Free your wives,
your children, the temples of your father's gods,
the burial places of your ancestors!
The time has come to fight for all of these!"

We responded with a confusing shout
from Persian tongues, but by now the crisis
left no time to delay. For right away,
the ships began to use their bronze-clad prows
to ram each other. In the first attack
a Greek ship completely smashed the bow   [410]
on a Phoenician boat, and after that
both rival navies went at one another.
At first, the bulk of the Persian forces
held them back. But with so many vessels
confined inside a narrow space, our ships
could provide no help to other Persians.
Instead their bronze prows rammed their own fleet's ships
and smashed the banks of oars. Meanwhile the Greeks
did not fail to seize this opportunity—
they formed a circle round us and attacked.
Our ships' hulls capsized, and the waves grew full
of shattered boats and slaughtered sailors,   [420]
so much so we could not glimpse the sea.
Beaches and rocks were crowded with the dead.
As all the ships left in our barbarian fleet
rushed off to escape in great confusion,
the Greeks kept butchering men in the sea,
hacking away at them with broken oars
and bits of wreckage, as if our sailors
were schools of mackerel or loads of fish.
Groans and screams of pain filled the open sea,
until night's shadowy eye concealed the scene.
But I could not describe the full extent   [430]
of the disaster to you, not even
if I spoke of it for ten entire days.
For you must understand that never before
has such an enormous multitude of men
all perished in a single day.

ΑΤΟΣΣΑ
αἰαῖ, κακῶν δὴ πέλαγος ἔρρωγεν μέγα
Πέρσαις τε καὶ πρόπαντι βαρβάρων γένει.

ΑΓΓΕΛΟΣ
εὖ νυν τόδ' ἴσθι, μηδέπω μεσοῦν κακόν·   435
τοιάδ' ἐπ' αὐτοῖς ἦλθε συμφορὰ πάθους
ὡς τοῖσδε καὶ δὶς ἀντισηκῶσαι ῥοπῇ.

ΑΤΟΣΣΑ
καὶ τίς γένοιτ' ἂν τῆσδ' ἔτ' ἐχθίων τύχη;
λέξον τίν' αὖ φὴς τήνδε συμφορὰν στρατῷ
ἐλθεῖν κακῶν ῥέπουσαν ἐς τὰ μάσσονα.   440

ΑΓΓΕΛΟΣ
Περσῶν ὅσοιπερ ἦσαν ἀκμαῖοι φύσιν,
ψυχήν τ' ἄριστοι κεὐγένειαν ἐκπρεπεῖς,
αὐτῷ τ' ἄνακτι πίστιν ἐν πρώτοις ἀεί,
τεθνᾶσιν αἰσχρῶς δυσκλεεστάτῳ μόρῳ.

ΑΤΟΣΣΑ
οἲ 'γὼ τάλαινα συμφορᾶς κακῆς, φίλοι.   445
ποίῳ μόρῳ δὲ τούσδε φὴς ὀλωλέναι;

ΑΓΓΕΛΟΣ
νῆσός τις ἔστι πρόσθε Σαλαμῖνος τόπων,
βαιά, δύσορμος ναυσίν, ἣν ὁ φιλόχορος
Πὰν ἐμβατεύει, ποντίας ἀκτῆς ἔπι.
ἐνταῦθα πέμπει τούσδ', ὅπως, ὅταν νεῶν   450
φθαρέντες ἐχθροὶ νῆσον ἐκσῳζοίατο,
κτείνοιεν εὐχείρωτον Ἑλλήνων στρατόν,
φίλους δ' ὑπεκσῴζοιεν ἐναλίων πόρων,
κακῶς τὸ μέλλον ἱστορῶν. ὡς γὰρ θεὸς
ναῶν ἔδωκε κῦδος Ἕλλησιν μάχης,   455

36

ATOSSA

Alas!
An immense sea of evil has engulfed
the Persians and our whole barbarian race!

MESSENGER

But listen—there is more. I have not mentioned
half our troubles yet. For our men suffered
evils twice as heavy as the ones before.

ATOSSA

What troubles worse than what you have described
could have hurt our army? Speak! You talked of
some catastrophe. What could have happened
to sink our scale of evil even further?   [440]

MESSENGER

All those Persians in their prime of life,
the very finest spirits, whose noble birth
made them exceptional, the foremost men,
who always had the trust of our Great King,
have met a most dishonourable fate
and died in shame.

ATOSSA

O my friends, this disaster
compounds my misery! What kind of fate
do you say killed these splendid men?

MESSENGER

There is an island in front of Salamis—
a tiny place, but hazardous for ships.[15]
Dance-loving Pan lives there, close to the shore.
Xerxes had placed his finest warriors here,   [450]
so that, when our defeated enemies
moved from the ships and sought a refuge
on that island, his men could overwhelm
the Grecian force where it was vulnerable,
and they could save the lives of any friends
trapped in the sea within that narrow strait.
But Xerxes' judgment of events was wrong.
For when some god gave glory to the Greeks
in the battle out at sea, that very day

37

αὐθημερὸν φράξαντες εὐχάλκοις δέμας
ὅπλοισι ναῶν ἐξέθρωσκον· ἀμφὶ δὲ
κυκλοῦντο πᾶσαν νῆσον, ὥστ᾽ ἀμηχανεῖν
ὅποι τράποιντο. πολλὰ μὲν γὰρ ἐκ χερῶν
πέτροισιν ἠράσσοντο, τοξικῆς τ᾽ ἄπο   460
θώμιγγος ἰοὶ προσπίτνοντές ὤλλυσαν·
τέλος δ᾽ ἐφορμηθέντες ἐξ ἑνὸς ῥόθου
παίουσι, κρεοκοποῦσι δυστήνων μέλη,
ἕως ἁπάντων ἐξαπέφθειραν βίον.
Ξέρξης δ᾽ ἀνώμωξεν κακῶν ὁρῶν βάθος·   465
ἕδραν γὰρ εἶχε παντὸς εὐαγῆ στρατοῦ,
ὑψηλὸν ὄχθον ἄγχι πελαγίας ἁλός·
ῥήξας δὲ πέπλους κἀνακωκύσας λιγύ,
πεζῷ παραγγείλας ἄφαρ στρατεύματι,
ἵησ᾽ ἀκόσμῳ ξὺν φυγῇ. τοιάνδε σοι   470
πρὸς τῇ πάροιθε συμφορὰν πάρα στένειν.

ΑΤΟΣΣΑ

ὦ στυγνὲ δαῖμον, ὡς ἄρ᾽ ἔψευσας φρενῶν
Πέρσας· πικρὰν δὲ παῖς ἐμὸς τιμωρίαν
κλεινῶν Ἀθηνῶν ηὗρε, κοὐκ ἀπήρκεσαν
οὓς πρόσθε Μαραθὼν βαρβάρων ἀπώλεσεν·   475
ὧν ἀντίποινα παῖς ἐμὸς πράξειν δοκῶν
τοσόνδε πλῆθος πημάτων ἐπέσπασεν.
σὺ δ᾽ εἰπέ, ναῶν αἳ πεφεύγασιν μόρον,
ποῦ τάσδ᾽ ἔλειπες· οἶσθα σημῆναι τορῶς;

ΑΓΓΕΛΟΣ

ναῶν γε ταγοὶ τῶν λελειμμένων σύδην   480
κατ᾽ οὖρον οὐκ εὔκοσμον αἴρονται φυγήν·
στρατὸς δ᾽ ὁ λοιπὸς ἔν τε Βοιωτῶν χθονὶ
διώλλυθ᾽, οἱ μὲν ἀμφὶ κρηναῖον γάνος
δίψῃ πονοῦντες, οἱ δ᾽ ὑπ᾽ ἄσθματος κενοὶ

they walled themselves in armour made of bronze,
leapt out of their ships, and formed a circle
around the island, so that our soldiers
had nowhere to escape. Many of our men
were hit with stones thrown by enemy hands   [460]
or died from falling arrows shot from bows.
At last in one concerted charge, the Greeks
attacked, hacking away at Persian limbs
until the lives of all those pitiful men
had been utterly destroyed. From high up
on a promontory right beside the sea
Xerxes watched. He had an excellent view
of his entire army, and, as he looked
and witnessed the extent of this defeat,
he groaned, tore his robes, gave out a shrill cry,
and quickly issued orders to his troops,
who ran away confused. This defeat   [470]
and the other one I talked of earlier—
these are the disasters you must grieve.

ATOSSA

O hateful demon, how you have deceived
the Persians! That famous city Athens
has taken harsh revenge against my son—
not satisfied with those barbarians
she killed at Marathon in years gone by.
By seeking retribution for those men,
my son has brought himself a multitude
of grief. What about the ships that got away?
Tell me where you left them. And do you have
a clear idea of where they might be now?

MESSENGER

Those in charge of our surviving ships   [480]
quickly fled away in great disorder,
on whatever course the winds might take them.
The remnants of our army was destroyed
in lands of the Boeotians—some of them
near a refreshing spring where they had gone,
driven there by thirst. Others among us,
exhausted and short of breath, kept marching

διεκπερῶμεν ἔς τε Φωκέων χθόνα 485
καὶ Δωρίδ᾽ αἶαν, Μηλιᾶ τε κόλπον, οὗ
Σπερχειὸς ἄρδει πεδίον εὐμενεῖ ποτῷ·
κἀντεῦθεν ἡμᾶς γῆς Ἀχαιίδος πέδον
καὶ Θεσσαλῶν πόλεις ὑπεσπανισμένους
βορᾶς ἐδέξαντ᾽· ἔνθα δὴ πλεῖστοι ᾽θάνον 490
δίψῃ τε λιμῷ τ᾽· ἀμφότερα γὰρ ἦν τάδε.
Μαγνητικὴν δὲ γαῖαν ἔς τε Μακεδόνων
χώραν ἀφικόμεσθ᾽, ἐπ᾽ Ἀξίου πόρον,
Βόλβης θ᾽ ἕλειον δόνακα, Πάγγαιόν τ᾽ ὄρος,
Ἠδωνίδ᾽ αἶαν· νυκτὶ δ᾽ ἐν ταύτῃ θεὸς 495
χειμῶν᾽ ἄωρον ὦρσε, πήγνυσιν δὲ πᾶν
ῥέεθρον ἁγνοῦ Στρυμόνος. θεοὺς δέ τις
τὸ πρὶν νομίζων οὐδαμοῦ τότ᾽ ηὔχετο
λιταῖσι, γαῖαν οὐρανόν τε προσκυνῶν.
ἐπεὶ δὲ πολλὰ θεοκλυτῶν ἐπαύσατο 500
στρατός, περᾷ κρυσταλλοπῆγα διὰ πόρον·
χὤστις μὲν ἡμῶν πρὶν σκεδασθῆναι θεοῦ
ἀκτῖνας ὡρμήθη, σεσωσμένος κυρεῖ.
φλέγων γὰρ αὐγαῖς λαμπρὸς ἡλίου κύκλος
μέσον πόρον διῆκε, θερμαίνων φλογί. 505
πῖπτον δ᾽ ἐπ᾽ ἀλλήλοισιν· ηὐτύχει δέ τοι
ὅστις τάχιστα πνεῦμ᾽ ἀπέρρηξεν βίου.
ὅσοι δὲ λοιποὶ κἄτυχον σωτηρίας,
Θρῄκην περάσαντες μόγις πολλῷ πόνῳ,
ἥκουσιν ἐκφυγόντες, οὐ πολλοί τινες, 510
ἐφ᾽ ἑστιοῦχον γαῖαν· ὡς στένειν πόλιν
Περσῶν, ποθοῦσαν φιλτάτην ἥβην χθονός.
ταῦτ᾽ ἔστ᾽ ἀληθῆ· πολλὰ δ᾽ ἐκλείπω λέγων
κακῶν ἃ Πέρσαις ἐγκατέσκηψεν θεός.

into Phocean land—reaching Doris
and the Gulf of Malia, where Spercheios
pours his fresh waters on the plain. And then,
desperate for food, we kept moving on
to the Achaean plain, where we were welcomed
by Thessalians in their cities. But here,
most of our men died of thirst or hunger,   [490]
for we were suffering from both. From there,
we reached the place where the Magnesians live
and Macedonian land—the river Axios,
Bolbe's reed-filled marsh, and Mount Pangaeon,
on Edonian ground.[16] But during the night
some spirit stirred up winter before its time.
The stream of the sacred river Strymon
was completely frozen, and all those men
who had given the gods no thought till then
at that point offered up their solemn prayers
with supplications to both Earth and Heaven.
Once the army had finished calling out   [500]
its many invocations to the gods,
we moved on across the frozen river.
Some of us, those who left before the god
could scatter his rays, crossed the ice in safety,
but once the brilliant circle of the sun
with his hot beams had warmed the middle part
and melted it with fire, then men fell through,
stumbling against each other. And the man
who lost the breath of life most rapidly
was truly lucky. The ones who got across
saved themselves by moving on through Thrace,
though not without much pain and suffering.
Not many of those fugitives escaped   [510]
and reached their native land. Now is the time
our Persian city should lament its loss,
grieving for the most cherished youthful men
in all our land. What I have said is true.
But I have left out many dreadful things
which a god has hurled down on the Persians.

[Exit Messenger]

Aeschylus

ΧΟΡΟΣ

ὦ δυσπόνητε δαῖμον, ὡς ἄγαν βαρὺς   515
ποδοῖν ἐνήλου παντὶ Περσικῷ γένει.

ΑΤΟΣΣΑ

οἲ 'γὼ τάλαινα διαπεπραγμένου στρατοῦ·
ὦ νυκτὸς ὄψις ἐμφανὴς ἐνυπνίων,
ὡς κάρτα μοι σαφῶς ἐδήλωσας κακά.
ὑμεῖς δὲ φαύλως αὔτ' ἄγαν ἐκρίνατε.   520
ὅμως δ', ἐπειδὴ τῇδ' ἐκύρωσεν φάτις
ὑμῶν, θεοῖς μὲν πρῶτον εὔξασθαι θέλω·
ἔπειτα Γῇ τε καὶ φθιτοῖς δωρήματα
ἥξω λαβοῦσα πέλανον ἐξ οἴκων ἐμῶν,—
ἐπίσταμαι μὲν ὡς ἐπ' ἐξειργασμένοις,   525
ἀλλ' ἐς τὸ λοιπὸν εἴ τι δὴ λῷον πέλοι.
ὑμᾶς δὲ χρὴ 'πὶ τοῖσδε τοῖς πεπραγμένοις
πιστοῖσι πιστὰ ξυμφέρειν βουλεύματα·
καὶ παῖδ', ἐάν περ δεῦρ' ἐμοῦ πρόσθεν μόλῃ,
παρηγορεῖτε, καὶ προπέμπετ' ἐς δόμους,   530
μὴ καί τι πρὸς κακοῖσι προσθῆται κακόν.

ΧΟΡΟΣ

ὦ Ζεῦ βασιλεῦ, νῦν ⟨γὰρ⟩ Περσῶν
τῶν μεγαλαύχων καὶ πολυάνδρων
στρατιὰν ὀλέσας
ἄστυ τὸ Σούσων ἠδ' Ἀγβατάνων   535
πένθει δνοφερῷ κατέκρυψας·
πολλαὶ δ' ἀταλαῖς χερσὶ καλύπτρας
κατερεικόμεναι
διαμυδαλέοις δάκρυσι κόλπους
τέγγουσ', ἄλγους μετέχουσαι.   540
αἱ δ' ἁβρόγοοι Περσίδες ἀνδρῶν
ποθέουσαι ἰδεῖν ἀρτιζυγίαν,

42

CHORUS LEADER

    O savage demon! With what heavy weight
    your feet have stamped on all the Persian race!

ATOSSA

    This overpowers me—the utter ruin
    of our entire force! Those visions last night—
    the ones I saw so clearly in my dreams—
    how plainly they revealed these blows to me.
    Your sense of them was far too trivial.   [520]
    But nonetheless, following your advice,
    I will begin by praying to the gods,
    and then I will return, bringing offerings
    for the Earth and for the dead—a libation
    from my home. I know I will be worshipping
    after all that has already happened,
    but I am hoping better things will come
    to us in future. Given these events,
    you men should demonstrate your loyalty
    by offering me trustworthy counsel.
    And if, while I am gone, my son arrives,
    comfort him, accompany him back home,   [530]
    so no misfortune comes to trouble him,
    apart from those we have already faced.

[Exit Atossa]

CHORUS LEADER

    O Zeus, king, now you have destroyed
    the overconfident armed multitude
    of the Persian army, shrouding
    the cities of Susa and Agbatana
    in gloom and overwhelming sorrow.
    And many women share our grief,
    ripping their veils with gentle hands,   [540]
    soaking their bosoms drenched in tears.
    With agonizing female cries
    the wives of Persia yearn to see
    those men they married only recently.

λέκτρων εὐνὰς ἁβροχίτωνας,
χλιδανῆς ἥβης τέρψιν, ἀφεῖσαι,
πενθοῦσι γόοις ἀκορεστοτάτοις.   545
κἀγὼ δὲ μόρον τῶν οἰχομένων
αἴρω δοκίμως πολυπενθῆ.

— νῦν γὰρ δὴ πρόπασα μὲν στένει γαῖ᾽
Ἀσιὰς ἐκκενουμένα.
Ξέρξης μὲν ἄγαγεν, ποποῖ,   550
Ξέρξης δ᾽ ἀπώλεσεν, τοτοῖ,
Ξέρξης δὲ πάντ᾽ ἐπέσπε δυσφρόνως
βαρίδεσσι ποντίαις.
τίπτε Δαρεῖος μὲν οὔ-
τω τότ᾽ ἀβλαβὴς ἐπῆν   555
τόξαρχος πολιήταις,
Σουσίδαις φίλος ἄκτωρ;

πεζούς τε γὰρ καὶ θαλασσίους
λινόπτεροι κυανώπιδες
νᾶες μὲν ἄγαγον, ποποῖ,   560
νᾶες δ᾽ ἀπώλεσαν, τοτοῖ,
νᾶες πανωλέθροισιν ἐμβολαῖς,
αἵ τ᾽ Ἰαόνων χέρες.
τυτθὰ δ᾽ ἐκφυγεῖν ἄνακτ᾽
αὐτὸν εἰσακούομεν   565
Θρήκης ἂμ πεδιήρεις
δυσχίμους τε κελεύθους.

τοὶ δ᾽ ἄρα πρωτόμοιροι, φεῦ,
λειφθέντες πρὸς ἀνάγκας, ἠέ,
ἀκτὰς ἀμφὶ Κυχρείας, ὀᾶ,   570
⟨σύρονται⟩· στένε καὶ δακνά-
ζου, βαρὺ δ᾽ ἀμβόασον
οὐράνι᾽ ἄχη, ὀᾶ·
τεῖνε δὲ δυσβάυκτον
βοᾶτιν τάλαιναν αὐδάν.   575

γναπτόμενοι δὲ δίνᾳ, φεῦ,
σκύλλονται πρὸς ἀναύδων, ἠέ,
παίδων τᾶς ἀμιάντου, ὀᾶ.

44

They leave their wedding beds,
the softly quilted joys of youth,
and howl with grief that has no end.
And I, in great distress, take on myself
the dreadful fate of those who are now gone.

CHORUS

Now indeed all lands in Asia
mourn their absent men!
Xerxes marched them off to war, alas!   [550]
Xerxes, to our sorrow, killed our men!
Xerxes, in his folly, took them all
and set out with a seagoing fleet.
Why then did Darius, while he lived
and ruled our city's archer armies,
remain unhurt and so well loved
by those who dwell in Susa?

Our troops on foot and sailors left
in the dark-eyed ships—alas!—   [560]
and went away on linen wings.[17]
Then other ships destroyed them,
obliterating all with their assault
at the hands of Ionian sailors.
And as we hear, our king himself
escaped, but only just, through Thrace,
on frozen paths across the plains.

Lament for those who perished earlier,
abandoned by necessity—alas!—
along Cychrean shores.[18] Such grief!   [570]
Scream out your sorrow, clench your teeth,
let cries of anguished mourning
climb the heights of heaven—alas!—
draw out your long and piteous moans.

They are torn by the deadly surf—alas!—
and gnawed by those voiceless children
of unpolluted seas—alas!

45

πενθεῖ δ' ἄνδρα δόμος στερη-
θείς τοκέες τ' ἄπαιδες 580
δαιμόνι' ἄχη, ὀᾶ,
δυρόμενοι γέροντες
τὸ πᾶν δὴ κλύουσιν ἄλγος.

τοὶ δ' ἀνὰ γᾶν Ἀσίαν δὴν
οὐκέτι περσονομοῦνται, 585
οὐδ' ἔτι δασμοφοροῦσιν
δεσποσύνοισιν ἀνάγκαις,
οὐδ' ἐς γᾶν προπίτνοντες
ἄζονται· βασιλεία
γὰρ διόλωλεν ἰσχύς. 590

οὐδ' ἔτι γλῶσσα βροτοῖσιν
ἐν φυλακαῖς· λέλυται γὰρ
λαὸς ἐλεύθερα βάζειν,
ὡς ἐλύθη ζυγὸν ἀλκᾶς.
αἱμαχθεῖσα δ' ἄρουραν 595
Αἴαντος περικλύστα
νᾶσος ἔχει τὰ Περσᾶν.

ΑΤΟΣΣΑ

φίλοι, κακῶν μὲν ὅστις ἔμπειρος κυρεῖ,
ἐπίσταται βροτοῖσιν ὡς ὅταν κλύδων
κακῶν ἐπέλθῃ πάντα δειμαίνειν φιλεῖ· 600
ὅταν δ' ὁ δαίμων εὐροῇ, πεποιθέναι
τὸν αὐτὸν αἰεὶ δαίμον' οὐριεῖν τύχην.
ἐμοὶ γὰρ ἤδη πάντα μὲν φόβου πλέα
ἐν ὄμμασιν τἀνταῖα φαίνεται θεῶν,
βοᾷ δ' ἐν ὠσὶ κέλαδος οὐ παιώνιος· 605
τοία κακῶν ἔκπληξις ἐκφοβεῖ φρένας.
τοιγὰρ κέλευθον τήνδ' ἄνευ τ' ὀχημάτων
χλιδῆς τε τῆς πάροιθεν ἐκ δόμων πάλιν

46

The grieving household mourns
its absent lord, and parents   [580]
whose children now are dead
cry out against the heaven-sent pain,
while the old, in sorrow, hear
of those men's agonies in full.

Now other men in Asian lands
no longer will abide by Persian laws,
no longer pay the Persians tribute,
under compulsion from our king.
No longer will they fall down prostrate
on the ground and worship him.
For the power of our king is gone!   [590]

No more will people check their tongues,
for now they have the liberty
to speak their minds without restraint.
The yoke of force has been removed,
and on that isle where Ajax ruled,
the blood-soaked rocks, washed by the sea,
now hold the power of Persia.

[Enter Atossa, this time without an escort]

ATOSSA

My friends, whoever has experienced disaster
understands that when a wave of trouble
breaks over mortal men, they are inclined   [600]
to be afraid of everything, and then,
when good fortune blows their way once more,
they start believing that this same good luck
will keep on blowing them success forever.
In my case, all things now look full of dread.
My eyes can see the gods are enemies,
and in my ears echoes a sound that brings
no note of joy. I am so overwhelmed
by these disasters—they have made my mind
so anxious and afraid. And that is why
I come here from the palace once again
without my chariots, without that pomp

Aeschylus

ἔστειλα, παιδὸς πατρὶ πρευμενεῖς χοὰς
φέρουσ', ἅπερ νεκροῖσι μειλικτήρια,				610
βοός τ' ἀφ' ἁγνῆς λευκὸν εὔποτον γάλα,
τῆς τ' ἀνθεμουργοῦ στάγμα, παμφαὲς μέλι,
λιβάσιν ὑδρηλαῖς παρθένου πηγῆς μέτα,
ἀκήρατόν τε μητρὸς ἀγρίας ἄπο
ποτὸν παλαιᾶς ἀμπέλου γάνος τόδε·			615
τῆς τ' αἰὲν ἐν φύλλοισι θαλλούσης βίον
ξανθῆς ἐλαίας καρπὸς εὐώδης πάρα,
ἄνθη τε πλεκτά, παμφόρου γαίας τέκνα,
ἀλλ', ὦ φίλοι, χοαῖσι ταῖσδε νερτέρων
ὕμνους ἐπευφημεῖτε, τόν τε δαίμονα			620
Δαρεῖον ἀνακαλεῖσθε, γαπότους δ' ἐγὼ
τιμὰς προπέμψω τάσδε νερτέροις θεοῖς.

ΧΟΡΟΣ
βασίλεια γύναι, πρέσβος Πέρσαις,
σύ τε πέμπε χοὰς θαλάμους ὑπὸ γῆς,
ἡμεῖς θ' ὕμνοις αἰτησόμεθα				625
φθιμένων πομποὺς
εὔφρονας εἶναι κατὰ γαίας.

ἀλλά, χθόνιοι δαίμονες ἁγνοί,
Γῆ τε καὶ Ἑρμῆ, βασιλεῦ τ' ἐνέρων,
πέμψατ' ἔνερθεν ψυχὴν ἐς φῶς·				630
εἰ γάρ τι κακῶν ἄκος οἶδε πλέον,
μόνος ἂν θνητῶν πέρας εἴποι.

— ἦ ῥ' ἀίει μου μακαρίτας
ἰσοδαίμων βασιλεὺς
βάρβαρ' ἀσαφηνῆ					635
ἱέντος τὰ παναίολ' αἰ-
ανῆ δύσθροα βάγματ', ἢ
παντάλαν' ἄχη διαβοάσω;
νέρθεν ἆρα κλύει μου;

48

I used to have before, bringing offerings
for the father of my son, libations
to propitiate and appease the dead—   [610]
sweet white milk from an unblemished cow
and splendid honey, distilled from flowers
by the bees, with water from a virgin spring,
and from their rustic mother earth I bring
this unmixed drink, the delightful produce
of the ancient vine, and this sweet-smelling fruit
from the plant whose leaves are always green,
the golden olive, with wreaths of flowers.
But you, my friends, should chant a choral song   [620]
to summon up the spirit of Darius,
while I pour these libations to the dead
and make an offering for the earth to drink,
in honour of the gods who rule below.

CHORUS LEADER

O royal lady, whom Persians all revere,
pour out your offerings to the earth beneath,
down to the chambers of the dead, while we
in song will beg those gods who guide
the dead down there to treat us kindly.

O you sacred gods of the world beneath,
Earth and Hermes, and you, O ruling king
of those who perish, send that man's spirit   [630]
from down below up here into the light.[19]
For if he knows of any further help
in our misfortunes, of all mortal men
he is the only one who can advise us
how to bring that remedy to bear.

CHORUS

Our sacred, godlike king,
does he attend to me,
as my obscure barbarian voice
sends out these riddling, wretched cries.
I will bewail my dreadful sorrow.
Does he hear me down below?

49

ἀλλὰ σύ μοι Γᾶ τε καὶ ἄλλοι   640
χθονίων ἀγεμόνες
δαίμονα μεγαυχῆ
ἰόντ᾽ αἰνέσατ᾽ ἐκ δόμων,
Περσᾶν Σουσιγενῆ θεόν·
πέμπετε δ᾽ ἄνω οἷον οὔπω   645
Περσὶς αἶ᾽ ἐκάλυψεν.

ἦ φίλος ἀνήρ, φίλος ὄχθος·
φίλα γὰρ κέκευθεν ἤθη.
Ἀιδωνεὺς δ᾽ ἀναπομ-
πὸς ἀνείης, Ἀιδωνεύς,   650
θεῖον ἀνάκτορα Δαριᾶνα. ἠέ.

οὐδὲ γὰρ ἄνδρας ποτ᾽ ἀπώλλυ
πολεμοφθόροισιν ἄταις,
θεομήστωρ δ᾽ ἐκικλή-
σκετο Πέρσαις, θεομήστωρ δ᾽   655
ἔσκεν,ἐπεὶ στρατὸν εὖ ποδούχει. ἠέ.

βαλήν, ἀρχαῖος βαλήν,
ἴθι, ἱκοῦ·
ἐλθ᾽ ἐπ᾽ ἄκρον κόρυμβον ὄχθου,
κροκόβαπτον ποδὸς εὔμαριν ἀείρων,   660
βασιλείου τιάρας
φάλαρον πιφαύσκων.
βάσκε πάτερ ἄκακε Δαριάν, οἶ.

ὅπως αἰανῆ κλύῃς
νέα τ᾽ ἄχη,   665
δέσποτα δεσπότου φάνηθι.
Στυγία γάρ τις ἐπ᾽ ἀχλὺς πεπόταται·
νεολαία γὰρ ἤδη
κατὰ πᾶσ᾽ ὄλωλεν.   670
βάσκε πάτερ ἄκακε Δαριάν, οἶ.

But you, O Earth, and you others,   [640]
you powers beneath the earth,
release his splendid spirit
from your homes—the divine one
born in Susa, the Persians' god.
Send him up here, that man whose like
was never laid to rest in Persian ground.

The man is loved, as is his tomb—
we love the virtue buried there.
O Aidoneus, Aidoneus,
who sends shades from the dead,   [650]
send Darius up here to us,
send back our godlike king.[20]

That ruler never lost our men
to ruinous death in war,
and Persians hailed him as divine
in his wise counsel, for, like a god,
when he led his army out to fight,
he planned things brilliantly. Alas!

O king, our old Great King,
approach us now, draw near.
Rise to the summit of your tomb,
lift up the saffron slipper on your foot,   [660]
reveal the royal ornaments
of your imperial crown,
and come to us, O father Darius,
who never caused us pain.

Come listen to our latest grief,
the sorrow felt throughout this land.
O king of Persia's king, appear.
For over us the darkness spreads,
a Stygian gloom, since our young men
have just been utterly destroyed.[21]   [670]
So come to us, O father Darius,
who never caused us pain.

Aeschylus

αἰαῖ αἰαῖ·
ὦ πολύκλαυτε φίλοισι θανών,
†τί τάδε δυνάτα δυνάτα   675
περὶ τᾷ σᾷ δίδυμα διαγόεν ἁμάρτια;†
πᾶσαι γᾷ τᾷδ᾽
ἐξέφθινται τρίσκαλμοι
νᾶες ἄναες ἄναες.   680

ΕΙΔΩΛΟΝ ΔΑΡΕΙΟΥ

ὦ πιστὰ πιστῶν ἥλικές θ᾽ ἥβης ἐμῆς
Πέρσαι γεραιοί, τίνα πόλις πονεῖ πόνον;
στένει, κέκοπται, καὶ χαράσσεται πέδον.
λεύσσων δ᾽ ἄκοιτιν τὴν ἐμὴν τάφου πέλας
ταρβῶ, χοὰς δὲ πρευμενὴς ἐδεξάμην.   685
ὑμεῖς δὲ θρηνεῖτ᾽ ἐγγὺς ἑστῶτες τάφου
καὶ ψυχαγωγοῖς ὀρθιάζοντες γόοις
οἰκτρῶς καλεῖσθέ μ᾽· ἐστὶ δ᾽ οὐκ εὐέξοδον,
ἄλλως τε πάντως χοὶ κατὰ χθονὸς θεοὶ
λαβεῖν ἀμείνους εἰσὶν ἢ μεθιέναι.   690
ὅμως δ᾽ ἐκείνοις ἐνδυναστεύσας ἐγὼ
ἥκω. τάχυνε δ᾽ ὡς ἄμεμπτος ὦ χρόνου.
τί ἐστι Πέρσαις νεοχμὸν ἐμβριθὲς κακόν·

ΧΟΡΟΣ

σέβομαι μὲν προσιδέσθαι,
σέβομαι δ᾽ ἀντία λέξαι   695
σέθεν ἀρχαίῳ περὶ τάρβει.

ΔΑΡΕΙΟΣ

ἀλλ᾽ ἐπεὶ κάτωθεν ἦλθον σοῖς γόοις πεπεισμένος,

52

Aaaaiii! Aaaiii!
O you whose death was mourned
so bitterly among your friends,
O great and powerful king,
[if you had been in full command
who in this land would now be grieving
such twin calamitous defeats?]²²
Our three-tiered ships—now ships no more—
have been completely overwhelmed.   [680]
Our ships are ships no more!

[The Ghost of Darius appears]

DARIUS

    You loyal men in whom I placed my trust,
    you ancient Persians, once my youthful friends,
    what troubles are now threatening the state?
    The soil is beaten down and torn apart—
    it groans in great distress. I see my wife
    beside my tomb, and so I grow concerned.
    I have received the offerings she made
    with favour, while you men have been standing here,
    close to my grave, chanting your laments,
    as with loud cries to summon up the dead
    you have been calling piteously for me.
    But there is no easy path from down below.
    Beneath the earth the gods are much more prone
    to welcome bodies than to send them back.   [690]
    Still, I do have some authority down there,
    and I have come. But you must not waste time,
    so I do not get blamed for my delay.
    What new disaster weighs the Persians down?

CHORUS

    That fear of you I had in earlier days
    makes me too awestruck now to look at you,
    and reverence inhibits what I say.

DARIUS

    But since I have responded to your cries
    and come up here from underneath the earth,

Aeschylus

μή τι μακιστῆρα μῦθον, ἀλλὰ σύντομον λέγων
εἰπὲ καὶ πέραινε πάντα, τὴν ἐμὴν αἰδῶ μεθείς.

ΧΟΡΟΣ

διέμαι μὲν χαρίσασθαι,   700
διέμαι δ' ἀντία φάσθαι,
λέξας δύσλεκτα φίλοισιν.

ΔΑΡΕΙΟΣ

ἀλλ' ἐπεὶ δέος παλαιὸν σοὶ φρενῶν ἀνθίσταται,
τῶν ἐμῶν λέκτρων γεραιὰ ξύννομ' εὐγενὲς γύναι,
κλαυμάτων λήξασα τῶνδε καὶ γόων σαφές τί μοι   705
λέξον· ἀνθρώπεια δ' ἄν τοι πήματ' ἂν τύχοι βροτοῖς.
πολλὰ μὲν γὰρ ἐκ θαλάσσης, πολλὰ δ' ἐκ χέρσου κακὰ
γίγνεται θνητοῖς, ὁ μάσσων βίοτος ἢν ταθῇ, πρόσω.

ΑΤΟΣΣΑ

ὦ βροτῶν πάντων ὑπερσχὼν ὄλβον εὐτυχεῖ πότμῳ
ὡς ἕως τ' ἔλευσσες αὐγὰς ἡλίου ζηλωτὸς ὢν   710
βίοτον εὐαίωνα Πέρσαις ὡς θεὸς διήγαγες,
νῦν τέ σε ζηλῶ θανόντα, πρὶν κακῶν ἰδεῖν βάθος.
πάντα γάρ, Δαρεῖ', ἀκούσῃ μῦθον ἐν βραχεῖ χρόνῳ.
διαπεπόρθηται τὰ Περσῶν πράγμαθ', ὡς εἰπεῖν ἔπος.

ΔΑΡΕΙΟΣ

τίνι τρόπῳ; λοιμοῦ τις ἦλθε σκηπτὸς ἢ στάσις πόλει;   715

ΑΤΟΣΣΑ

οὐδαμῶς· ἀλλ' ἀμφ' Ἀθήνας πᾶς κατέφθαρται στρατός.

ΔΑΡΕΙΟΣ

τίς δ' ἐμῶν ἐκεῖσε παίδων ἐστρατηλάτει; φράσον.

54

you must ignore the awe that I inspire
and speak. Tell me everything that has gone on.
But keep the details brief—no lengthy story.

CHORUS

I am afraid to act on your request,   [700]
too full of fear to speak directly to you
and say things hard to tell to those one loves.

DARIUS

Since ancient reverence affects your minds,

[*Turning toward Atossa*]

will you, noble and venerable queen,
who shared my bed, hold back your tears and groans
and speak quite frankly to me? We all know
that mortal blows will fall on mortal men.
Many from the sea, many from the land
afflict all human beings, as their long lives
keep stretching through the years.

ATOSSA

O you, whose happy fate made you surpass
all other men in your prosperity,
for as long as you gazed at the brilliant sun,   [710]
you lived a fortunate life men envied,
and Persians looked on you as on a god.
And now I envy you, for you have died
before you saw the depths of our misfortune.
O Darius, you will hear everything.
A few words tell it all—one might well say
the Persian state is utterly destroyed.

DARIUS

How is this so? Has our country suffered
from some foul pestilence or civil strife?

ATOSSA

No, not at all. But somewhere close to Athens
all our forces have been overpowered.

DARIUS

What son of mine led our armies there? Speak.

ΑΤΟΣΣΑ

θούριος Ξέρξης, κενώσας πᾶσαν ἠπείρου πλάκα.

ΔΑΡΕΙΟΣ

πεζὸς ἢ ναύτης δὲ πεῖραν τήνδ᾽ ἐμώρανεν τάλας;

ΑΤΟΣΣΑ

ἀμφότερα· διπλοῦν μέτωπον ἦν δυοῖν στρατευμάτοιν. 720

ΔΑΡΕΙΟΣ

πῶς δὲ καὶ στρατὸς τοσόσδε πεζὸς ἤνυσεν περᾶν;

ΑΤΟΣΣΑ

μηχαναῖς ἔζευξεν Ἕλλης πορθμόν, ὥστ᾽ ἔχειν πόρον.

ΔΑΡΕΙΟΣ

καὶ τόδ᾽ ἐξέπραξεν, ὥστε Βόσπορον κλῇσαι μέγαν·

ΑΤΟΣΣΑ

ὧδ᾽ ἔχει· γνώμης δέ πού τις δαιμόνων ξυνήψατο.

ΔΑΡΕΙΟΣ

φεῦ, μέγας τις ἦλθε δαίμων, ὥστε μὴ φρονεῖν καλῶς. 725

ΑΤΟΣΣΑ

ὡς ἰδεῖν τέλος πάρεστιν οἷον ἤνυσεν κακόν.

ΔΑΡΕΙΟΣ

καὶ τί δὴ πράξασιν αὐτοῖς ὧδ᾽ ἐπιστενάζετε;

ΑΤΟΣΣΑ

ναυτικὸς στρατὸς κακωθεὶς πεζὸν ὤλεσε στρατόν.

ATOSSA

    Impetuous Xerxes—he drained the men
    from our whole mainland plain.

DARIUS

                That reckless wretch!
    Did he launch this foolish expedition
    by land or sea?

ATOSSA

             By both. The double force
    proceeded on two fronts.   [720]

DARIUS

             How could the men,
    a group of infantry that size, succeed
    in moving past the Hellespont?

ATOSSA

                 Xerxes
    used a clever scheme to yoke the river
    and forge a way across.

DARIUS

            He managed this?
    He closed the mighty Bosporus?[23]

ATOSSA

                   He did.
    Some spirit must have helped him with his plan.

DARIUS

    Alas! Some mighty spirit came to him
    and stopped him thinking clearly.

ATOSSA

    Yes. And we can see the result of that,
    the enormous ruin his actions caused.

DARIUS

    Why do you grieve for them? What happened?

ATOSSA

    The destruction of our naval forces
    led to the slaughter of our men on land.

Aeschylus

ΔΑΡΕΙΟΣ

ὧδε παμπήδην δὲ λαὸς πᾶς κατέφθαρται δορί;

ΑΤΟΣΣΑ

πρὸς τάδ᾽ ὡς Σούσων μὲν ἄστυ πᾶν κενανδρίαν στένει. 730

ΔΑΡΕΙΟΣ

ὦ πόποι κεδνῆς ἀρωγῆς κἀπικουρίας στρατοῦ.

ΑΤΟΣΣΑ

Βακτρίων δ᾽ ἔρρει πανώλης δῆμος, οὐδέ τις γέρων.

ΔΑΡΕΙΟΣ

ὦ μέλεος, οἵαν ἄρ᾽ ἥβην ξυμμάχων ἀπώλεσεν.

ΑΤΟΣΣΑ

μονάδα δὲ Ξέρξην ἔρημόν φασιν οὐ πολλῶν μέτα—

ΔΑΡΕΙΟΣ

πῶς τε δὴ καὶ ποῖ τελευτᾶν; ἔστι τις σωτηρία; 735

ΑΤΟΣΣΑ

ἄσμενον μολεῖν γέφυραν γαῖν δυοῖν ζευκτηρίαν.

ΔΑΡΕΙΟΣ

καὶ πρὸς ἤπειρον σεσῶσθαι τήνδε, τοῦτ᾽ ἐτήτυμον;

ΑΤΟΣΣΑ

ναί· λόγος κρατεῖ σαφηνὴς τοῦτό γ᾽, οὐδ᾽ ἔνι στάσις.

ΔΑΡΕΙΟΣ

φεῦ, ταχεῖά γ᾽ ἦλθε χρησμῶν πρᾶξις, ἐς δὲ παῖδ᾽ ἐμὸν
Ζεὺς ἀπέσκηψεν τελευτὴν θεσφάτων· ἐγὼ δέ που 740
διὰ μακροῦ χρόνου τάδ᾽ ηὔχουν ἐκτελευτήσειν θεούς·

58

DARIUS

    And so the entire army came to grief,
    butchered by the spear?

ATOSSA

               Yes. And that is why
    all of Susa mourns—the entire city   [730]
    laments its missing men.

DARIUS

               Alas for the loss!
    The help and defence of the army gone!

ATOSSA

    All those troops from Bactria are now dead—
    not even an old man remains.

DARIUS

    O wretched Xerxes! So many allies!
    He has killed off all our youth!

ATOSSA

               The people say
    he is now by himself, with few attendants.

DARIUS

    How will this end? Do you have any hope
    he could be rescued?

ATOSSA

             There is some good news—
    he reached the bridge that links two continents.

DARIUS

    He returned to Asia safely? Is that true?

ATOSSA

    It is. We have had news confirming it
    beyond all doubt.

DARIUS

             Alas! Those oracles
    have quickly been proved true, and Zeus has let
    their full prophetic weight fall on my son.
    I had hoped the gods would somehow hold off   [740]
    fulfilling them for several years. But then,

ἀλλ' ὅταν σπεύδῃ τις αὐτός, χὠ θεὸς συνάπτεται.

νῦν κακῶν ἔοικε πηγὴ πᾶσιν ηὑρῆσθαι φίλοις.

παῖς δ' ἐμὸς τάδ' οὐ κατειδὼς ἤνυσεν νέῳ θράσει·

ὅστις Ἑλλήσποντον ἱρὸν δοῦλον ὣς δεσμώμασιν   745

ἤλπισε σχήσειν ῥέοντα, Βόσπορον ῥόον θεοῦ·

καὶ πόρον μετερρύθμιζε, καὶ πέδαις σφυρηλάτοις

περιβαλὼν πολλὴν κέλευθον ἤνυσεν πολλῷ στρατῷ,

θνητὸς ὢν θεῶν τε πάντων ᾤετ', οὐκ εὐβουλίᾳ,

καὶ Ποσειδῶνος κρατήσειν. πῶς τάδ' οὐ νόσος φρενῶν   750

εἶχε παῖδ' ἐμόν; δέδοικα μὴ πολὺς πλούτου πόνος

οὑμὸς ἀνθρώποις γένηται τοῦ φθάσαντος ἁρπαγή.

ΑΤΟΣΣΑ

ταῦτά τοι κακοῖς ὁμιλῶν ἀνδράσιν διδάσκεται

θούριος Ξέρξης· λέγουσι δ' ὡς σὺ μὲν μέγαν τέκνοις

πλοῦτον ἐκτήσω ξὺν αἰχμῇ, τὸν δ' ἀνανδρίας ὕπο   755

ἔνδον αἰχμάζειν, πατρῷον δ' ὄλβον οὐδὲν αὐξάνειν.

τοιάδ' ἐξ ἀνδρῶν ὀνείδη πολλάκις κλύων κακῶν

τήνδ' ἐβούλευσεν κέλευθον καὶ στράτευμ' ἐφ' Ἑλλάδα.

ΔΑΡΕΙΟΣ

τοιγάρ σφιν ἔργον ἐστὶν ἐξειργασμένον

μέγιστον, ἀείμνηστον, οἷον οὐδέπω   760

τόδ' ἄστυ Σούσων ἐξεκείνωσεν πεσόν,

ἐξ οὗτε τιμὴν Ζεὺς ἄναξ τήνδ' ὤπασεν,

when the man himself is in a hurry,
the god will take steps, too. It seems to me
a fountain of misfortunes has been found
for all the ones I love. It was my son
who, knowing nothing of these matters,
with his youthful rashness brought them on.
He wished to check the sacred Hellespont
by tying it down with chains, just like a slave,
and that holy river, too, the Bosporus.
He built a roadway never seen before,
enclosing it with hammered manacles,
creating there a generous causeway
for his enormous force. Though a mortal man,
he sought to force his will on all the gods,
a foolish scheme, even on Poseidon.[24]
Why do that? Surely a sickness of the mind   [750]
possessed my son? I fear that our great wealth,
amassed by my hard work, may well become
the spoils of anyone who marches here.

ATOSSA

Xerxes spent too much time with wicked men
and learned to be impulsive. They told him
how you had won great riches for your sons
by fighting with your spear, while he, in fear,
just used his spear at home and did not add
to the wealth his father left. Gibes like this,
which Xerxes often heard from evil men
led him to organize this expedition
and launch an armed campaign against the Greeks.

DARIUS

And so he has achieved his mighty deed,
the greatest of them all, truly immense,
whose memory will never be erased—   [760]
he has removed from Susa all its citizens,
something no man has ever done before,
not since the time our sovereign Zeus proclaimed

Aeschylus

ἔν᾽ ἄνδρ᾽ ἀπάσης Ἀσίδος μηλοτρόφου
ταγεῖν, ἔχοντα σκῆπτρον εὐθυντήριον.
Μῆδος γὰρ ἦν ὁ πρῶτος ἡγεμὼν στρατοῦ·   765
ἄλλος δ᾽ ἐκείνου παῖς τόδ᾽ ἔργον ἤνυσεν·
φρένες γὰρ αὐτοῦ θυμὸν ᾠακοστρόφουν.
τρίτος δ᾽ ἀπ᾽ αὐτοῦ Κῦρος, εὐδαίμων ἀνήρ,
ἄρξας ἔθηκε πᾶσιν εἰρήνην φίλοις·
Λυδῶν δὲ λαὸν καὶ Φρυγῶν ἐκτήσατο,   770
Ἰωνίαν τε πᾶσαν ἤλασεν βίᾳ.
θεὸς γὰρ οὐκ ἤχθηρεν, ὡς εὔφρων ἔφυ.
Κύρου δὲ παῖς τέταρτος ηὔθυνε στρατόν.
πέμπτος δὲ Μάρδος ἦρξεν, αἰσχύνη πάτρᾳ
θρόνοισί τ᾽ ἀρχαίοισι· τὸν δὲ σὺν δόλῳ   775
Ἀρταφρένης ἔκτεινεν ἐσθλὸς ἐν δόμοις,
ξὺν ἀνδράσιν φίλοισιν, οἷς τόδ᾽ ἦν χρέος.
ἕκτος δὲ Μάραφις, ἕβδομος δ᾽ Ἀρταφρένης.
κἀγὼ πάλου τ᾽ ἔκυρσα τοῦπερ ἤθελον,
κἀπεστράτευσα πολλὰ σὺν πολλῷ στρατῷ·   780
ἀλλ᾽ οὐ κακὸν τοσόνδε προσέβαλον πόλει.
Ξέρξης δ᾽ ἐμὸς παῖς ὢν νέος νέα φρονεῖ,
κοὐ μνημονεύει τὰς ἐμὰς ἐπιστολάς·
εὖ γὰρ σαφῶς τόδ᾽ ἴστ᾽, ἐμοὶ ξυνήλικες,
ἅπαντες ἡμεῖς, οἳ κράτη τάδ᾽ ἔσχομεν,   785
οὐκ ἂν φανεῖμεν πήματ᾽ ἔρξαντες τόσα.

ΧΟΡΟΣ

τί οὖν, ἄναξ Δαρεῖε, ποῖ καταστρέφεις
λόγων τελευτήν; πῶς ἂν ἐκ τούτων ἔτι
πράσσοιμεν ὡς ἄριστα Περσικὸς λεώς;

ΔΑΡΕΙΟΣ

εἰ μὴ στρατεύοισθ᾽ ἐς τὸν Ἑλλήνων τόπον,   790

62

one man should have the honour of being king
in all sheep-breeding Asia and should hold
the sceptre of imperial command.
Medos was the first to lead its armies,
and then another man, his son, who had
a spirit guided by intelligence,
finished the work his father had begun.[25]
Third after him was Cyrus, a leader
favoured by the gods, for his rule brought peace
to all his friends. He added to his realm
the Lydian and Phrygian people   [770]
and subdued all the Ionians by force.[26]
The god felt no hostility towards him,
because his mind was wise. A son of Cyrus
was the fourth in charge of Persia's armies,
and Mardos was the fifth, a man who shamed
his country and disgraced the ancient throne.
But noble Artaphrenes with the help
of comrades who undertook this duty
hatched a scheme and did away with Mardos
in his home. [Sixth in line was Maraphis,
and seventh Artaphrenes]. When my turn came,
I won the lot I wished for.[27] Many times
I led our mighty armies in campaigns,   [780]
and yet I never brought such great disaster
to our Persian state. But my son Xerxes,
who is still young, has immature ideas
and does not bear in mind what I advised.
For you whose old age matches mine know well
that none of us who have held ruling power
was ever seen to cause such great distress.

CHORUS LEADER

But then, lord Darius, these words of yours—
what do they imply? What do you conclude?
After these events, what should we Persians do
to serve this land the best way possible?

DARIUS

You must not organize armed expeditions   [790]
against Hellenic lands, not even if

63

Aeschylus

μηδ' εἰ στράτευμα πλεῖον τὸ Μηδικόν.
αὐτὴ γὰρ ἡ γῆ ξύμμαχος κείνοις πέλει.

ΧΟΡΟΣ

πῶς τοῦτ' ἔλεξας, τίνι τρόπῳ δὲ συμμαχεῖ;

ΔΑΡΕΙΟΣ

κτείνουσα λιμῷ τοὺς ὑπερπόλλους ἄγαν.

ΧΟΡΟΣ

ἀλλ' εὐσταλῆ τοι λεκτὸν ἀροῦμεν στόλον.   795

ΔΑΡΕΙΟΣ

ἀλλ' οὐδ' ὁ μείνας νῦν ἐν Ἑλλάδος τόποις
στρατὸς κυρήσει νοστίμου σωτηρίας.

ΧΟΡΟΣ

πῶς εἶπας; οὐ γὰρ πᾶν στράτευμα βαρβάρων
περᾷ τὸν Ἕλλης πορθμὸν Εὐρώπης ἄπο;

ΔΑΡΕΙΟΣ

παῦροί γε πολλῶν, εἴ τι πιστεῦσαι θεῶν   800
χρὴ θεσφάτοισιν, ἐς τὰ νῦν πεπραγμένα
βλέψαντα· συμβαίνει γὰρ οὐ τὰ μέν, τὰ δ' οὔ.
κεἴπερ τάδ' ἐστί, πλῆθος ἔκκριτον στρατοῦ
λείπει κεναῖσιν ἐλπίσιν πεπεισμένος.
μίμνουσι δ' ἔνθα πεδίον Ἀσωπὸς ῥοαῖς   805
ἄρδει, φίλον πίασμα Βοιωτῶν χθονί·
οὗ σφιν κακῶν ὕψιστ' ἐπαμμένει παθεῖν,
ὕβρεως ἄποινα κἀθέων φρονημάτων·

64

the Persian force is larger than before.
They have an ally—the very land itself.

CHORUS LEADER

What do you mean? In what way is the land
their ally?

DARIUS

Those armies which are very large
she kills with famine.

CHORUS LEADER

Then we will raise
some special soldiers and supply them well.

DARIUS

But that army which is still in Greece
will not get safely home.

CHORUS LEADER

What are you saying?
Will all our forces of barbarians
not make their way across the Hellespont
and out of Europe?

DARIUS

Not very many—
only a few of that huge multitude,   [800]
if, after those events we have been through,
we still place any trust in prophecies
the gods have made. For it is not the case
that some will be fulfilled and others not.
If the oracles are true, then Xerxes,
convinced by empty hopes, will leave behind
a specially chosen portion of his army,
now stationed where the river Asopus
waters the plains and brings Boeotian lands
sweet nourishment. This is the place those men
remain to undergo their punishment,
the very worst disaster of them all,
a payment for their pride and godless thoughts.

οἳ γῆν μολόντες Ἑλλάδ' οὐ θεῶν βρέτη

ᾐδοῦντο συλᾶν οὐδὲ πιμπράναι νεώς· 810

βωμοὶ δ' ἄιστοι, δαιμόνων θ' ἱδρύματα

πρόρριζα φύρδην ἐξανέστραπται βάθρων.

τοιγὰρ κακῶς δράσαντες οὐκ ἐλάσσονα

πάσχουσι, τὰ δὲ μέλλουσι, κοὐδέπω κακῶν

κρηνὶς ἀπέσβηκ' ἀλλ' ἔτ' ἐκπιδύεται. 815

τόσος γὰρ ἔσται πέλανος αἱματοσφαγὴς

πρὸς γῇ Πλαταιῶν Δωρίδος λόγχης ὕπο·

θῖνες νεκρῶν δὲ καὶ τριτοσπόρῳ γονῇ

ἄφωνα σημανοῦσιν ὄμμασιν βροτῶν

ὡς οὐχ ὑπέρφευ θνητὸν ὄντα χρὴ φρονεῖν. 820

ὕβρις γὰρ ἐξανθοῦσ' ἐκάρπωσεν στάχυν

ἄτης, ὅθεν πάγκλαυτον ἐξαμᾷ θέρος.

τοιαῦθ' ὁρῶντες τῶνδε τἀπιτίμια

μέμνησθ' Ἀθηνῶν Ἑλλάδος τε, μηδέ τις

ὑπερφρονήσας τὸν παρόντα δαίμονα 825

ἄλλων ἐρασθεὶς ὄλβον ἐκχέῃ μέγαν.

Ζεύς τοι κολαστὴς τῶν ὑπερκόμπων ἄγαν

φρονημάτων ἔπεστιν, εὔθυνος βαρύς.

πρὸς ταῦτ' ἐκεῖνον, σωφρονεῖν κεχρημένον,

πινύσκετ' εὐλόγοισι νουθετήμασιν, 830

λῆξαι θεοβλαβοῦνθ' ὑπερκόμπῳ θράσει.

σὺ δ', ὦ γεραιὰ μῆτερ ἡ Ξέρξου φίλη,

ἐλθοῦσ' ἐς οἴκους κόσμον ὅστις εὐπρεπὴς

λαβοῦσ' ὑπαντίαζε παιδί. πάντα γὰρ

κακῶν ὑπ' ἄλγους λακίδες ἀμφὶ σώματι 835

στημορραγοῦσι ποικίλων ἐσθημάτων.

For when they first arrived in Greece, those men
did not display the slightest reverence
but broke in pieces images of gods   [810]
and burned their temples. They ravaged altars
demolished holy shrines, knocking them down
to their foundations, leaving scattered ruins.
And thus, given their acts were so profane,
the evils they must suffer are no less—
and others are in store. They have not plumbed
the depths of their disasters—more troubles
will keep flowing yet. The mix of blood and gore
poured out by Dorian spears across the earth
of Plataea will be so great the dead,
the corpses heaped in piles, will still be there
when three generations have come and gone,
a silent witness to the eyes of men
that mortal human beings should not believe   [820]
that they are greater than they are.[28] For pride,
when it grows ripe, produces as its fruit
disastrous folly and a harvest crop
of countless tears. So when you look upon
the punishment for how these men behaved,
remember Greece and Athens. Do not let
any man despise the god he follows
and, in his lust for something else, squander
the great wealth he possesses. I tell you
Zeus does act to chastise arrogant men
whose thoughts are far too proud, and when he does
his hand is heavy. So now that Xerxes
has shown he lacks the prudence to think well,
you must teach him with sensible advice   [830]
to stop being so offensive to the gods
through his presumptuous daring. As for you,
dear lady, Xerxes' venerable mother,
return back to the palace. Pick out there
some clothing fit for him, and then prepare
to meet your son. His grief at his misfortune
has torn to shreds the embroidered clothing
covering his body. Use soothing words

67

ἀλλ' αὐτὸν εὐφρόνως σὺ πράυνον λόγοις·
μόνης γάρ, οἶδα, σοῦ κλύων ἀνέξεται.
ἐγὼ δ' ἄπειμι γῆς ὑπὸ ζόφον κάτω.
ὑμεῖς δέ, πρέσβεις, χαίρετ', ἐν κακοῖς ὅμως   840
ψυχῇ διδόντες ἡδονὴν καθ' ἡμέραν,
ὡς τοῖς θανοῦσι πλοῦτος οὐδὲν ὠφελεῖ.

ΧΟΡΟΣ
ἦ πολλὰ καὶ παρόντα καὶ μέλλοντ' ἔτι
ἤλγησ' ἀκούσας βαρβάροισι πήματα.

ΑΤΟΣΣΑ
ὦ δαῖμον, ὥς με πόλλ' ἐσέρχεται κακὰ   845
ἄλγη, μάλιστα δ' ἥδε συμφορὰ δάκνει,
ἀτιμίαν γε παιδὸς ἀμφὶ σώματι
ἐσθημάτων κλύουσαν, ἥ νιν ἀμπέχει.
ἀλλ' εἶμι, καὶ λαβοῦσα κόσμον ἐκ δόμων
ὑπαντιάζειν παιδί μου πειράσομαι.   850
οὐ γὰρ τὰ φίλτατ' ἐν κακοῖς προδώσομεν.

ΧΟΡΟΣ
ὦ πόποι ἦ μεγάλας ἀγαθᾶς τε πο-
λισσονόμου βιοτᾶς ἐπεκύρσαμεν,
εὖθ' ὁ γηραιὸς
πανταρκὴς ἀκάκας   855
ἄμαχος βασιλεὺς
ἰσόθεος Δαρεῖος ἆρχε χώρας.

πρῶτα μὲν εὐδοκίμους στρατιὰς ἀπε-
φαινόμεθ', ἡδὲ νομίσματα πύργινα
πάντ' ἐπηύθυνε,   860
νόστοι δ' ἐκ πολέμων
ἀπόνους ἀπαθεῖς
⟨ἀνέρας⟩ εὖ πράσσοντας ἆγον οἴκους.

ὅσσας δ' εἷλε πόλεις πόρον
οὐ διαβὰς Ἄλυος ποταμοῖο,   865
οὐδ' ἀφ' ἑστίας συθείς,

and gently calm him down, for I know this—
yours is the only voice he listens to.
As for me, I am returning to the earth,
to darkness down below. Farewell, old men,
despite these troubling times, you should each day   [840]
discover reasons to rejoice, for riches
bring no profit whatsoever to the dead.

[The Ghost of Darius disappears]

CHORUS LEADER
To hear about the many troubles
we barbarians must face, the ones
already here and still more yet to come,
fills me with grief.

ATOSSA
                    O god, I am overwhelmed
with so much bitter sorrow! But one thing
more than all the others gnaws my heart—
the disgraceful appearance of my son,
the shameful clothing covering his limbs.
But I will go and get appropriate robes
and try to find my son. In this distress,   [850]
I will not abandon those most dear to me.

[Atossa exits]

CHORUS
Alas! How glorious and good the life
we loved here in our well-run city,
when our old sovereign ruled this land,
our all-sufficient and unconquered king,
who never brought us war or grief,
our mighty godlike Darius.

For first of all, we then displayed
our famous armies, and our traditions,   [860]
like towers in strength, ruled everything.
Our men returning from a war
faced no disasters—they reached
their prosperous homes unharmed.

Darius seized so many cities
and never crossed the Halys stream
or even left his home—places like

69

οἶαι Στρυμονίου πελά-
γους Ἀχελωίδες εἰσὶ πάροικοι
Θρηκίων ἐπαύλων,   870

λίμνας τ' ἔκτοθεν αἳ κατὰ
χέρσον ἐληλαμέναι πέρι πύργον
τοῦδ' ἄνακτος ἄιον,
Ἕλλας τ' ἀμφὶ πόρον πλατὺν   875
εὐχόμεναι, μυχία τε Προποντίς,
καὶ στόμωμα Πόντου·

νᾶσοί θ' αἳ κατὰ πρῶν'
ἅλιον περίκλυστοι   880
τᾷδε γᾷ προσήμεναι
οἵα Λέσβος ἐλαι-
όφυτός τε Σάμος, Χίος
ἠδὲ Πάρος, Νάξος, Μύκο-
νος, Τήνῳ τε συνάπτουσ'   885
Ἄνδρος ἀγχιγείτων,

καὶ τὰς ἀγχιάλους
ἐκράτυνε μεσάκτους,
Λῆμνον, Ἰκάρου θ' ἕδος,   890
καὶ Ρόδον ἠδὲ Κνίδον
Κυπρίας τε πόλεις, Πάφον,
ἠδὲ Σόλους, Σαλαμῖνά τε,
τᾶς νῦν ματρόπολις τῶνδ'   895
αἰτία στεναγμῶν.

καὶ τὰς εὐκτεάνους κατὰ
κλῆρον Ἰαόνιον πολυάνδρους
Ἑλλάνων ἐκράτει σφετέραις φρεσίν.   900
ἀκάματον δὲ παρῆν σθένος
ἀνδρῶν τευχηστήρων
παμμίκτων τ' ἐπικούρων.
νῦν δ' οὐκ ἀμφιλόγως
θεότρεπτα τάδ' αὖ   905
φέρομεν πολέμοισι
δμαθέντες μεγάλως
πλαγαῖσι ποντίαισιν.

the Thracian Acheloan towns
beside the Strymonian sea.²⁹ [870]

And cities on the mainland, too,
far from the sea, well fortified
with walls encircling them
obeyed him as their king,
and so did places on both shores
along the spacious Hellespont
and in the deep bays of Propontis
and where the Pontus flows into the sea.³⁰

And islands close to coastal headlands,
surrounded by the sea, right next to us,
like Lesbos, Samos, where olives grow,
and Chios, Paros, Naxos,
Mykonos, along with Andros, too,
adjacent to its neighbour Teos.

He ruled the wave-washed isles, as well,
which lie far out at sea—Lemnos,
the home of Icarus, and Rhodes,
with Cnidus, too, and Cyprian cities—
Paphos and Soli and Salamis,
whose mother state has caused
our present cries of anguish.³¹

And wealthy crowded cities of those Greeks
descended from Ionian stock
he ruled with his shrewd mind, [900]
and under his command he had
enormous armies of warrior men—
all nations were allied with him.
But now we must endure defeats
in wars inflicted by the gods.
We cannot doubt the truth of this,
for we have been destroyed in war,
by massive disaster on the sea.

71

ΞΕΡΞΗΣ
ἰώ,
δύστηνος ἐγὼ στυγερᾶς μοίρας
τῆσδε κυρήσας ἀτεκμαρτοτάτης,　910
ὡς ὠμοφρόνως δαίμων ἐνέβη
Περσῶν γενεᾷ· τί πάθω τλήμων;
λέλυται γὰρ ἐμοὶ γυίων ῥώμη
τήνδ᾽ ἡλικίαν ἐσιδόντ᾽ ἀστῶν.
εἴθ᾽ ὄφελεν, Ζεῦ, κἀμὲ μετ᾽ ἀνδρῶν　915
τῶν οἰχομένων
θανάτου κατὰ μοῖρα καλύψαι.

ΧΟΡΟΣ
ὀτοτοῖ, βασιλεῦ, στρατιᾶς ἀγαθῆς
καὶ περσονόμου τιμῆς μεγάλης,
κόσμου τ᾽ ἀνδρῶν,　920
οὓς νῦν δαίμων ἐπέκειρεν.
γᾶ δ᾽ αἰάζει τὰν ἐγγαίαν
ἥβαν Ξέρξᾳ κταμέναν Ἅιδου
σάκτορι Περσᾶν. ἀδοβάται γὰρ
πολλοὶ φῶτες, χώρας ἄνθος,　925
τοξοδάμαντες, πάνυ ταρφύς τις
μυριὰς ἀνδρῶν, ἐξέφθινται.
αἰαῖ αἰαῖ κεδνᾶς ἀλκᾶς.
Ἀσία δὲ χθών, βασιλεῦ γαίας,
αἰνῶς αἰνῶς　930
ἐπὶ γόνυ κέκλιται.

ΞΕΡΞΗΣ
ὅδ᾽ ἐγώ, οἰοῖ, αἰακτὸς
μέλεος γέννᾳ γᾷ τε πατρῴᾳ
κακὸν ἄρ᾽ ἐγενόμαν.

ΧΟΡΟΣ
πρόσφθογγόν σοι νόστου τὰν　935
κακοφάτιδα βοάν,
κακομέλετον ἰὰν
Μαριανδυνοῦ θρηνητῆρος
πέμψω πέμψω,
πολύδακρυν ἰαχάν.　940

[Enter Xerxes]

XERXES

    O my situation now is desperate!

    My luck has led me to a cruel fate   [910]

    which I did not foresee! How savagely

    a demon trampled on the Persian race.

    What must I still endure in this distress?

    As I look on these ancient citizens,

    the strength in my limbs fails. O how I wish

    a fatal doom from Zeus had buried me

    with all those men who perished!

CHORUS LEADER

                   Alas, my king,

    for our brave force and the mighty honour

    of Persia's influence, those splendid men   [920]

    whom fate has now cut down. The earth laments

    her native youth, the soldiers Xerxes killed,

    who filled all Hades with the Persian dead.

    So many men—our country's flowers—slain,

    thousands perishing from enemy bows,

    a close-packed multitude, all dead and gone.

    Alas! Alas, for all our brave protectors!

    O sovereign of the earth, all Asian lands

    are now upon their knees, a dreadful sight,   [930]

    so dreadful. . . .

XERXES

           You see me here, alas, a sad

    and useless wretch who has become

    an evil presence for my race

    and for my native land.

CHORUS

    For your return I will send out

    in these harsh-sounding tones

    a cry of ominous grief,

    one full of tears, a shout

    of Mariandynian sorrow.[32]   [940]

ΞΕΡΞΗΣ
ἵετ᾽ αἰανῆ καὶ πάνδυρτον   941
δύσθροον αὐδάν. δαίμων γὰρ ὅδ᾽ αὖ
μετάτροπος ἐπ᾽ ἐμοί.

ΧΟΡΟΣ
ἥσω τοι τὰν πάνδυρτον,
σὰ πάθη τε σέβων   945
ἁλίτυπά τε βάρη,
πόλεως γέννας πενθητῆρος·
⟨κλάγξω⟩ κλάγξω
δὲ γόον ἀρίδακρυν.

ΞΕΡΞΗΣ
Ἰάνων γὰρ ἀπηύρα,   950
Ἰάνων ναύφρακτος
Ἄρης ἑτεραλκὴς
νυχίαν πλάκα κερσάμενος
δυσδαίμονά τ᾽ ἀκτάν.

ΧΟΡΟΣ
οἰοιοῖ βόα καὶ πάντ᾽ ἐκπεύθου.—   955
ποῦ δὲ φίλων ἄλλος ὄχλος,
ποῦ δέ σοι παραστάται,
οἷος ἦν Φαρανδάκης,
Σούσας, Πελάγων, καὶ Δοτάμας, ἠδ᾽ Ἀ-
γδαβάτας, Ψάμμις, Σουσισκάνης τ᾽   960
Ἀγβάτανα λιπών;

ΞΕΡΞΗΣ
ὀλοοὺς ἀπέλειπον
Τυρίας ἐκ ναὸς
ἔρροντας ἐπ᾽ ἀκταῖς
Σαλαμινιάσι στυφελοῦ   965
θείνοντας ἐπ᾽ ἀκτᾶς.

ΧΟΡΟΣ
οἰοιοῖ, ⟨βόα⟩· ποῦ σοι Φαρνοῦχος
Ἀριόμαρδός τ᾽ ἀγαθός,
ποῦ δὲ Σευάλκης ἄναξ,
ἢ Λίλαιος εὐπάτωρ,   970

74

XERXES

> Then let your sad lament resound,
> a harsh and plaintive cry.
> For the god has turned against me.

CHORUS

> Yes, I will sing my tearful chant
> to honour the men who suffered so
> in that defeat at sea—a dirge
> from those who mourn this land
> and lament its slaughtered sons.
> My doleful grief I voice once more.

XERXES

> Ionian Ares with those ships of war   [950]
> turned the tide of victory
> and swept our troops away—
> the Greek fleet razed the murky sea
> and that fatal cliff onshore.

CHORUS

> Aaaaiii! Cry out your sorrows,
> and learn the tale in full.
> Where are they now, that multitude
> of other friends so dear to us?
> Where are the ones who stood by you—
> Pharandaces, and Sousas, and Pelagon,
> with Agabatas and Dotamas,
> Psammis, and Sousiskanes,   [960]
> who came from Agbatana?

XERXES

> I left them there. They perished,
> tumbling out of their Tyrian ship
> by the coast of Salamis,
> beaten against its rugged shore.

CHORUS

> Aaaiii! Where is Pharnouchus, your friend,
> and Ariomardus, that glorious man?
> And lord Seualcus or Lilaios,
> descended from a noble line,   [970]

75

Μέμφις, Θάρυβις, καὶ Μασίστρας,
Ἀρτεμβάρης τ' ἠδ' Ὑσταίχμας;
τάδε σ' ἐπανερόμαν.

ΞΕΡΞΗΣ
ἰὼ ἰώ μοί μοι
τὰς ὠγυγίους κατιδόντες   975
στυγνὰς Ἀθάνας πάντες ἑνὶ πιτύλῳ,
ἐὴ ἐή, τλάμονες ἀσπαίρουσι χέρσῳ.

ΧΟΡΟΣ
ἦ καὶ τὸν Περσᾶν αὐτοῦ
τὸν σὸν πιστὸν πάντ' ὀφθαλμὸν
μυρία μυρία πεμπαστὰν   980
Βατανώχου παῖδ' Ἄλπιστον
τοῦ Σησάμα τοῦ Μεγαβάτα,
Πάρθον τε μέγαν τ' Οἰβάρην
ἔλιπες ἔλιπες;
ὢ ὢ <ὢ> δᾴων.   985
Πέρσαις ἀγαυοῖς κακὰ πρόκακα λέγεις.

ΞΕΡΞΗΣ
<ἰὼ ἰὼ> δῆτα
ἴυγγ' ἀγαθῶν ἑτάρων μοι ὑπομιμνήσκεις
<κινεῖς> ἄλαστα στυγνὰ πρόκακα λέγων.   990
βοᾷ βοᾷ <μοι> μελέων ἔντοσθεν ἦτορ.

ΧΟΡΟΣ
καὶ μὴν ἄλλους γε ποθοῦμεν,
Μάρδων ἀνδρῶν μυριοταγὸν
Ξάνθιν ἄρειόν τ' Ἀγχάρην,
Δίαιξίν τ' ἠδ' Ἀρσάκην   995
ἱππιάνακτας,
Κηγδαδάταν καὶ Λυθίμναν
Τόλμον τ' αἰχμᾶς ἀκόρεστον.

or Memphis, Tharybis, and Masistras,
or Hystaichmas and Artembares?
I am asking you about them, too.

XERXES

Alas! Alas! They caught a glimpse
of ancient Athens, that hateful place!
Now all of them at one fell blow—
the pain of those poor wretches!—
lie gasping on the shore.

CHORUS

And did you really leave behind
Alpistos, son of Batanochus,
your ever loyal Persian eye
who tracked men by the thousands?   [980]
[. . . . .]33
The sons of Sesames and Megabates,
with Parthos and the great Oibares—
did you abandon them, as well,
and leave them with the others?
Alas, alas, for those poor men!
You talk of catastrophic woes
among our noble Persians.

XERXES

What you say truly makes me yearn
for all my fine companions,
when you bring up the evil times,   [990]
that hateful woe I cannot bear.
From deep within, my grieving heart
howls out my pain and sorrow.

CHORUS

But there are other men we miss—
like Xanthes, who as commander
captained countless Mardian men,
as well as warlike Anchares,
and Diaixis, too, and Arsakes,
who led the cavalry,
and Agdadatas, Lythimnas,
and Tolmus, too, whose appetite
could never get enough of war.

ἔταφον ἔταφον,
οὐκ ἀμφὶ σκηναῖς   1000
τροχηλάτοισιν ὄπιθεν δ' ἑπομένους.

ΞΕΡΞΗΣ
βεβᾶσι γὰρ τοίπερ ἀγρέται στρατοῦ.

ΧΟΡΟΣ
βεβᾶσιν, οἵ, νώνυμοι.

ΞΕΡΞΗΣ
ἰὴ ἰή, ἰὼ ἰώ.

ΧΟΡΟΣ
ἰὼ ἰώ, δαίμονες,   1005
ἔθεθ' ἄελπτον κακὸν
διαπρέπον, οἷον δέδορκεν Ἄτα.

ΞΕΡΞΗΣ
πεπλήγμεθ' οἵᾳ δι' αἰῶνος τύχᾳ·   1008

ΧΟΡΟΣ
πεπλήγμεθ'· εὔδηλα γάρ·

ΞΕΡΞΗΣ
νέᾳ νέᾳ δύᾳ δύᾳ.   1010

ΧΟΡΟΣ
κύρσαντες οὐκ εὐτυχῶς   1012
Ἰάνων ναυβατᾶν.   1011
δυσπόλεμον δὴ γένος τὸ Περσᾶν.   1013

ΞΕΡΞΗΣ
πῶς δ' οὔ; στρατὸν μὲν τοσοῦ-
τον τάλας πέπληγμαι.   1015

ΧΟΡΟΣ
τί δ' οὔκ; ὄλωλεν μεγάλως τὰ Περσᾶν.

I am amazed they are not here
marching behind you in your train
with your wheel-drawn carriage tent.

[1000]

XERXES

Those leaders of our forces are all dead.

CHORUS

They are gone? Alas! And with no glory!

XERXES

Aaaaiiii! The sorrow!

CHORUS

Alas! Alas, you spirits above,
you bring us such disaster,
so unforeseen and yet so clear to see,
as if the goddess of folly, Ate,
had glanced at us in this calamity.34

XERXES

We have been hit by blows,
smitten by unexpected blows of fate!

CHORUS

Yes, all too clearly stricken!

XERXES

New troubles, strange disasters!

[1010]

CHORUS

It was bad luck for us we ran into
those ships and sailors from Ionia.
The Persian race, as we can see,
has had no luck in war.

XERXES

How can that be? Such a mighty force!
And I, a miserable wretch,
have now been beaten down!

CHORUS

And of our splendid Persian glory
what has not perished?

Aeschylus

ΞΕΡΞΗΣ
ὁρᾷς τὸ λοιπὸν τόδε τᾶς ἐμᾶς στολᾶς;

ΧΟΡΟΣ
ὁρῶ ὁρῶ.

ΞΕΡΞΗΣ
τόνδε τ' οἰστοδέγμονα—   1020

ΧΟΡΟΣ
τί τόδε λέγεις σεσωσμένον;

ΞΕΡΞΗΣ
θησαυρὸν βελέεσσιν;

ΧΟΡΟΣ
βαιά γ' ὡς ἀπὸ πολλῶν.

ΞΕΡΞΗΣ
ἐσπανίσμεθ' ἀρωγῶν.

ΧΟΡΟΣ
Ἰάνων λαὸς οὐ φυγαίχμας.   1025

ΞΕΡΞΗΣ
ἀγανόρειος· κατεῖ-
δον δὲ πῆμ' ἄελπτον.

ΧΟΡΟΣ
τραπέντα ναύφρακτον ἐρεῖς ὅμιλον;

ΞΕΡΞΗΣ
πέπλον δ' ἐπέρρηξ' ἐπὶ συμφορᾷ κακοῦ.   1030

ΧΟΡΟΣ
παπαῖ παπαῖ.

ΞΕΡΞΗΣ
καὶ πλέον ἢ παπαῖ μὲν οὖν.

XERXES

Do you see my robes—
what's left of them?

CHORUS

Yes, I see . . . I see them now.

XERXES

And my quiver here . . .   [1020]

CHORUS

What are you saying?
Is this what has been saved?

XERXES

. . . this holder for my arrows?

CHORUS

So small a remnant from so many!

XERXES

We have lost all our protectors!

CHORUS

Ionian troops are not afraid to fight.

XERXES

They are a warlike race. I witnessed there
what I did not expect—a great defeat.

CHORUS

You mean the way they beat your warships—
that massive fleet?

XERXES

When that disaster came,
I ripped my clothing.

CHORUS

Alas! Alas!

XERXES

And there were even more catastrophes
to make one cry "Alas!"

ΧΟΡΟΣ
δίδυμα γάρ ἐστι καὶ τριπλᾶ—

ΞΕΡΞΗΣ
λυπρά, χάρματα δ᾽ ἐχθροῖς.

ΧΟΡΟΣ
καὶ σθένος γ᾽ ἐκολούσθη—   1035

ΞΕΡΞΗΣ
γυμνός εἰμι προπομπῶν.

ΧΟΡΟΣ
φίλων ἄταισι ποντίαισιν·

ΞΕΡΞΗΣ
δίαινε δίαινε πῆμα· πρὸς δόμους δ᾽ ἴθι.

ΧΟΡΟΣ
αἰαῖ αἰαῖ, δύα δύα.

ΞΕΡΞΗΣ
βόα νυν ἀντίδουπά μοι.   1040

ΧΟΡΟΣ
δόσιν κακὰν κακῶν κακοῖς.

ΞΕΡΞΗΣ
ἴυζε μέλος ὁμοῦ τιθείς.

ΧΟΡΟΣ
ὀτοτοτοτοῖ.
βαρεῖά γ᾽ ἅδε συμφορά.
οἲ μάλα καὶ τόδ᾽ ἀλγῶ.   1045

ΞΕΡΞΗΣ
ἔρεσσ᾽ ἔρεσσε καὶ στέναζ᾽ ἐμὴν χάριν.

ΧΟΡΟΣ
διαίνομαι γοεδνὸς ὤν.

CHORUS

                      Two and three times more!

XERXES

    Crushing grief—but for our enemies great joy!

CHORUS

    Our strength has been lopped off.

XERXES

    I am now naked—stripped of my attendants!

CHORUS

    By deaths of friends who perished on the sea.

XERXES

    Weep for that catastrophe! Let your tears fall.
    Then return back to your homes.

CHORUS

                    Alas, such grief!
    Alas, for our distress!

XERXES

                Your cries of sorrow—
    let them echo mine!   [1040]

CHORUS

    An answering cry of anguished pain
    from one grief to another.

XERXES

    Cry out and link together our laments!

CHORUS

    Aaaaiiii! Misfortunes hard to bear!
    For I too share your grief!

XERXES

    For my sake beat your chests and groan!

CHORUS

    My sorrow drenches me with tears!

ΞΕΡΞΗΣ
βόα νυν ἀντίδουπά μοι.

ΧΟΡΟΣ
μέλειν πάρεστι, δέσποτα.

ΞΕΡΞΗΣ
ἐπορθίαζέ νυν γόοις.   1050

ΧΟΡΟΣ
ὀτοτοτοτοῖ.
μέλαινα δ᾽ ἀμμεμείξεται,
οἵ, στονόεσσα πλαγά.

ΞΕΡΞΗΣ
καὶ στέρν᾽ ἄρασσε κἀπιβόα τὸ Μύσιον.

ΧΟΡΟΣ
ἄνι᾽ ἄνια.   1055

ΞΕΡΞΗΣ
καί μοι γενείου πέρθε λευκήρη τρίχα.

ΧΟΡΟΣ
ἄπριγδ᾽ ἄπριγδα μάλα γοεδνά.

ΞΕΡΞΗΣ
ἀύτει δ᾽ ὀξύ.

ΧΟΡΟΣ
καὶ τάδ᾽ ἔρξω.

ΞΕΡΞΗΣ
πέπλον δ᾽ ἔρεικε κολπίαν ἀκμῇ χερῶν.   1060

ΧΟΡΟΣ
ἄνι᾽ ἄνια.

ΞΕΡΞΗΣ
καὶ ψάλλ᾽ ἔθειραν καὶ κατοίκτισαι στρατόν.

ΧΟΡΟΣ
ἄπριγδ᾽ ἄπριγδα μάλα γοεδνά.

84

XERXES

Shout out your cries to answer mine.

CHORUS

We will respond to you, my king.

XERXES

Now raise your voices high in your laments.   [1050]

CHORUS

Aaaaaiiiii! Once more
we mix our song of grief
with these dark blows of pain!

XERXES

Now beat your chests and as you do
howl out a Mysian strain!

CHORUS

                                                Such grief! Such sorrow!

XERXES

And tear those white hairs on your chin!

CHORUS

With fists I clench my beard and moan!

XERXES

Let your shrill cries ring out!

CHORUS

                                                I will cry out!

XERXES

And with your fingers rip your flowing robes!   [1060]

CHORUS

                                                The pain! The sorrow!

XERXES

Now tug your hair out as you cry
for our lost army!

CHORUS

                                With these fists
I clench my hair and moan!

ΞΕΡΞΗΣ
διαίνου δ᾽ ὄσσε.

ΧΟΡΟΣ
τέγγομαί τοι.   1065

ΞΕΡΞΗΣ
βόα νυν ἀντίδουπά μοι.

ΧΟΡΟΣ
οἰοῖ οἰοῖ.

ΞΕΡΞΗΣ
αἰακτὸς ἐς δόμους κίε.

ΧΟΡΟΣ
ἰὼ ἰώ, Περσὶς αἶα δύσβατος.   1070

ΞΕΡΞΗΣ
ἰωὰ δὴ κατ᾽ ἄστυ.

ΧΟΡΟΣ
ἰωὰ δῆτα, ναὶ ναί.

ΞΕΡΞΗΣ
γοᾶσθ᾽ ἁβροβάται.

ΧΟΡΟΣ
ἰὼ ἰώ, Περσὶς αἶα δύσβατος.

ΞΕΡΞΗΣ
ἰὴ ἰὴ τρισκάλμοισιν,
ἰὴ ἰή, βάρισιν ὀλόμενοι.   1075

ΧΟΡΟΣ
πέμψω τοί σε δυσθρόοις γόοις.

86

XERXES

Let your eyes fill with tears.

CHORUS

They do! They do!

XERXES

Shout out your cries to answer mine.

CHORUS

Alas! Alas!

XERXES

And now, as you lament, go home.

CHORUS

Alas! Alas! Such grief to move   [1070]
across our Persian land.

XERXES

Such grief throughout the city.

CHORUS

So much pain, so much distress!

XERXES

Tread softly as you wail your grief.

CHORUS

Alas! Alas! Such grief to move
across our Persian land.

XERXES

Aaaaiii! Alas, for those destroyed
in the flat bottomed boats—
the power of those three-tiered galleys!

CHORUS

I will be your escort and attend on you
with mournful cries of sorrow.

[Xerxes and the Chorus exit]

NOTES

1. The name Atossa is not mentioned in the Greek manuscripts, but the name is well known.

2. It is not totally clear from the text whether the building is the royal palace or a special council building or something else entirely.

3. The mainland referred to is Asia Minor (as opposed to the islands). Many cities in this region, especially along the coast, were part of the Persian Empire but inhabited by Ionians, that is, by Greeks closely related to the Athenians. The Greek cities resented Persian rule and had rebelled against it in the past. The three- or four-horse teams mentioned refers to the number of horses who rode abreast. Lydia is a region in Asia Minor. Tmolus is a mountain near the Persian city of Sardis. The Mysians came from northern Asia Minor. Greek traditions stressed the enormous size of Xerxes' forces. Herodotus' (no doubt exaggerated) claim puts the number of soldiers and army followers at over three million.

4. One of the two narrow straits separating Asia from Europe was named after Helle, a daughter of Athamas, who fell from the sky and drowned in the water there. Xerxes led his immense army across this obstacle on a bridge made of boats. The boats were tied together with cables and chains, and then planks and earth were placed on top to make a roadway. A Persian fleet accompanied the army.

5. Atossa's entry here is probably meant to be imperially splendid, with chariots and an impressive escort, in contrast to her entry later in the play. There is no sense that she enters from the building at the back.

6. The Dorians were an ethnic group within the Greek people (and frequent rivals of the Ionians). They were commonly associated with Sparta, the most important Dorian city.

7. Hellenic means Greek. The word barbarian, a term the Greeks used to refer to non-Greeks, is here a reference to Persia.

8. The terms Mede and Persian were, for the Greeks, synonymous. The Athenians were the most important element in the Greek force which had defeated Darius' expeditionary army at Marathon ten years earlier

(in 490 BC). Some editors believe that two lines are missing immediately before this passage, another question from Atossa and an answer from the Chorus.

9. Attica, the region around Athens, had very profitable silver mines.

10. Salamis is an island in the Saronic Gulf, close to Athens. It was famous for its sailors. Once Xerxes' army entered Greece, it was at first successful, moving past Thermopylae down into central Greece and raising alarm in Athens and elsewhere. The Athenians, placing their faith in their formidable navy, abandoned the city and moved to Salamis with their fleet.

11. This reference to the battle of Marathon ten years before emphasizes the vital role played by the Athenians in the combined Greek force which defeated the army Darius has sent.

12. The name Ajax refers to the Greater Ajax, king of Salamis, who in the *Iliad* is the mightiest Greek warrior at Troy after Achilles.

13. Pallas is a reference to Athena, the patron goddess of Athens. The city of Athens had, in fact, been ravaged by the Persian army, which occupied the city, because the citizens had abandoned the town and gone to Salamis and Aegina.

14. The phrase *envy of the gods* refers to the belief that the gods were jealous of a mortal being's success and punished him for it, especially when the display of his greatness became excessive.

15. The island was called Psytteleia.

16. After the battle the Persian land forces moved north, away from Salamis, to make their way back to Asia Minor. The places listed are more or less in geographical order.

17. Ships often had eyes painted on their prows to make them look like sea creatures.

18. The phrase Cychrean shores is a reference to Salamis.

19. The ruler of the underworld is Hades, brother of Zeus and Poseidon. The spirit the Chorus wishes to conjure up is, of course, Darius.

20. Aidoneus is an alternative name for Hades, god of the dead.

21. The word Stygian refers to the Styx, a major river in the underworld.

22. The precise meaning of these lines is not altogether clear.

23. The Hellespont (now called the Dardanelles) and the Bosporus are the two straits which separate Asia from Europe in Asia Minor. For Aeschylus both names refer to the westernmost strait (i.e., the Hellespont). At its narrowest point, this strait is about half a mile across.

24. Poseidon, a brother of Zeus and Hades, was god of the sea.

25. That is, he succeeded in bringing a large part of Asia under Persian rule. The Greek word *Medos* may not be a proper name but simply mean "a Mede."

26. Lydia and Phrygia were areas in Asia Minor near the Mediterranean coast. The term Ionians here refers to the Greeks in Asia Minor and some adjacent islands. It does not include the Ionians elsewhere.

27. These lines refer to the traditional story that when the Persian nobles who conspired against Mardos succeeded, they drew lots to determine the imperial succession. In different accounts of this event, the names of the conspirators and the succeeding kings differ. Line 778 in the Greek is generally considered an interpolation (hence the square brackets).

28. Darius is here referring to the great land battle of Plataea, in Boeotia, where the Greek forces led by the Spartans, who were of Dorian descent, defeated the Persian land armies, after the naval battle of Salamis.

29. It is not entirely clear what places these phrases refer to, since the meaning of the Greek word *Acheloan* is disputed. The Halys River in Lydia, the longest river in Asia Minor, marked (for the Greeks) the western boundary of Persia.

30. The Propontis (now called the Sea of Marmora) is a large body of water between the Bosporus and the Hellespont. Pontus was normally the name of a region on the south shores of the Black Sea. Here is seems to apply to a river or rivers in the area.

31. Icarus, son of Daedalus, attempted to fly away from Crete on wings his father, Daedalus, had made. But when he flew too near the sun, the wax holding his feathers melted, and he fell into the sea and drowned. The Icarian Sea in the eastern Mediterranean was named after him.

32. The Mariandynians were a Thracian people, famous for their funeral laments.

33. The "eyes" of the Persian king were officials whose task was to keep him informed about what was going on among the king's subjects. Some portion of the text is evidently missing after line 981 in the Greek.

34. Ate, the goddess of folly, caused people temporarily to lose all their judgment, so that they made decisions with disastrous consequences.

Made in the USA
Middletown, DE
01 May 2021